It's Not What You Say

mastering the art of powerful communication

bill cakmis

LOST
COAST
PRESS
Fort Bragg
California

Y0-BZH-145

IT'S NOT WHAT YOU SAY:
MASTERING THE ART OF POWERFUL COMMUNICATION
Copyright ©2001 by Bill Cakmis

Lost Coast Press
155 Cypress Street
Fort Bragg, CA 95437
(800) 773-7782
www.cypresshouse.com

Cover design and illustration:
Charles Hathaway / Mendocino Graphics

ISBN 1-882897-58-7   LCCN 00-134216

Manufactured in the U.S.A.
First edition
2   4   6   8   9   7   5   3   1

About the Author

BILL CAKMIS IS AN ACCOMPLISHED DIRECTOR, writer, actor, consultant, and teacher. He has trained, advised, and developed actors and communicators in all fields of the entertainment and broadcast news industries since 1980. Bill's writing accomplishments include the long-running hit play *Circle of Will*, which garnered the *LA Weekly* Pick of the Week, *The LA Times* "Calendar" section Pick of the Week, and the *LA Weekly* Theatre Award for Best Comedy Writing of 1986. He was also staff writer and researcher for the interactive, multi-media educational program, "Columbus: Discovery and Beyond."

Bill has directed more than thirty plays, dramatic readings, and musicals, in Equity and Non-Equity theatres and universities across the country. He received the Long Beach Playhouse Directing Award for "Best Play of the Season," and has directed many West Coast premiers, including *Early One Evening at the Rainbow Bar and Grille*, *At the Bluff*, and *Bad Soldiers*. In the Dallas/Fort Worth metro-plex, he directed musicals including *The Sound of Music* and *The Wizard of Oz*, thereby raising funds for charitable organizations and programs supporting children in the arts.

Bill has appeared in eight films, six episodics, four daytime serials, and twenty stage productions. He is a member of the Screen Actor's Guild (SAG) and the American Federation of Television and Radio Artists (AFTRA).

Bill's client list as a talent coach and consultant includes on-screen personalities, politicians, lawyers, directors, producers, writers, athletes, news stations, production companies, networks, and studios. In addition to working privately, he has conducted classes and seminars on interpersonal and group communications and intermediate and advanced level acting/directing classes in such venues as the National Leadership Training Centers, The Beverly Hills Playhouse, The Actor's Studio, Jacksonville University, and KD Studios in Dallas. Bill is currently a senior talent consultant for the Media Advisors International family of companies, including ASI Entertainment, Audience Research & Development, and Talent Dynamics.

For Dru-Anne
She is, therefore I am

ACKNOWLEDGMENTS

I MUST GRATEFULLY ACKNOWLEDGE two colleagues for their support: Lynn Gartley, vice-president of Talent Dynamics, and Jim Willi, president of Audience Research and Development, have both been valiant champions of this project, and extremely helpful as editors and counselors.

As I interviewed many talented, creative individuals for this project, there were, in addition to those included in this volume, people who offered invaluable aid and were most generous with their time, including: Bill Taylor, Sandra Connell, JJ Davis, Caryn Richman, RAC Clark, Carmen Argenziano, Tim Hopper, David Ruprecht, and Jack Grapes.

A special word of thanks to Florence M. Sikes: For the last twenty-five years, Flo has been a mentor, a comrade-in-arms, an inspiration and a good friend. She has shed light on the path toward mastery for many students over the years, and I consider myself blessed for having been one of them.

CONTENTS

PROLOGUE

THE LOOK
OF LOVE

"THE EYES ARE THE WINDOWS TO THE SOUL."

DURING MY BRIEF TENURE AS A PROFESSIONAL ACTOR in the late seventies and early eighties, I had the good fortune to work with some honest-to-goodness "stars," as well as a few "personality" types. These opportunities afforded many life-lessons that did not always relate to my "craft." One such experience occurred while working on a project with a young woman named Patti Davis. Patti had seen my work on stage and approached me to do a scene with her for an acting class.

In those days, preparation and rehearsals for a scene-study project in that particular venue could take up to six weeks. There were the "get to know you" meetings, the "When are we going to meet?" meetings, the "discussion of scene and characters" meetings, the "shopping for props and stuff" meetings and, of course, the actual rehearsal meetings. For a concentrated period of time, an acting partner would become an integral part of your life (which is why it's always necessary to choose acting partners with a careful eye toward compatibility).

During our first meeting, I found Patti to be amiable, intelligent, and possessing a quirky sense of humor that I found quite interesting and fun, so I quickly agreed to her request. It never occurred to me at the time that working with Patti, who also happened to be Ronald Reagan's daughter, might present its own unique set of problems. Well, you live and learn.

At that time, Mr. Reagan was the president of the United States. Subsequently, no matter where Patti and I were when we were alone together—sitting in a restaurant booth, riding in a car, visiting in each other's apartments—there was an ominous feeling that we were always being watched. That is, of course, because we *were* always being watched! Secret Service men were everywhere, never more than fifty yards away. I'm sure their directive was to be "invisible," but if you looked closely, like searching for Waldo in the funny papers, you could spot these guys—lurking, parked in sedans, hanging outside my apartment, camped inside hers. It was, to say the least, disquieting.

Patti was always a bit embarrassed and aggravated with her "shadows." Often, she felt the need to apologize or explain them away. They represented a part of her life she wasn't particularly proud of. She knew she needed them, but the admission of their existence was maddening, and while she would express humor at the circumstances, her misery was palpable. I became frustrated with the whole situation after having had to deal with it for a mere few weeks (though I could have sworn they were tapping my phone for months afterward). I could only imagine Patti's aggravation after living with it for years.

I had a great deal of fun working with Patti and getting to know her as a person. But what I'll never forget was the look in her eyes each time she spoke about those clandestine guardians. She would give them a labored glance that expressed the wry, yet painful, acceptance of a necessary evil. It was an uncomfortable situation that I hoped I'd never have to witness again. Which is why I was so dismayed when, a year later at one of the many Hollywood awards banquets, I recognized that same look from one of the celebrities as I unintentionally overheard him speaking in hushed tones to a friend . . . about his acting coach!

How was it possible?! I couldn't understand then why a celebrated artist would attempt to explain away his association with a mentor who had worked diligently to help him achieve a higher level of dynamics in his craft and, ultimately, an award for the success that had previously eluded him. I'm sure the coach in question was paid quite well for his efforts, but witnessing a fellow teacher being publicly shrugged off was disheartening.

Yes, I was much younger then. Now that I'm older, it's still disheartening, but it is understandable. I've seen that look again and again over the years as I watched professionals reluctantly discuss with others their need for a coach, teacher, or consultant. Thankfully, it isn't always the case, but many professionals regard coaching as Patti regarded her secret service guards: they know they need it, but despise having to endure it. They appreciate the counsel and are usually amazed at the substantial growth, which they readily attribute to the coach's tutelage. On the other hand, they find it embarrassing and frustrating if they can't be as good as they want to be through their own use of positive thinking, transcendental meditation, becoming vegetarian, or taking some other autodidactic approach.

If investigated, the backgrounds of our great artists, athletes, and leaders would reveal that most were inspired early on by a coach or instructor. The phrase "Those who can't do, teach." is an unenlightened sentiment, and one that has probably relegated teachers in our society to the low-paying, under-appreciated positions they find themselves in today. Is it really necessary that Olympic coaches be physically superior to the athletes they work with? Should only a Michelangelo be allowed to instruct other artists or an Einstein other scientists? Wouldn't it be wonderful if we were all gifted in every field? But then there would be no need for teachers. The fact of the matter is, a Master's brilliant abilities are rarely coupled with brilliant teaching skills.

Future history books will probably rate Jaime Escalante as one of the great 20th-century American teachers. He is best known from the 1988 feature film *Stand and Deliver*, which depicts his efforts to raise academic standards at a predominantly Hispanic high school in East Los Angeles, by striving to train his students to take the Advanced Placement Calculus Test. Jaime's unorthodox method of teaching and his unrelenting pursuit of excellence resulted in the school ranking fourth in the country in the number of students taking that exam. Years ago, I had the opportunity to speak with Jaime, and asked him about his desire to be a teacher. He told me that his inspiration and fascination with teaching came from his mother, who had been a teacher in Bolivia. Apparently, his unconventional teaching style came from watching her unique techniques—like having the children pull apart navel oranges to learn about fractions. She told her son, "If I give you money, it will soon be gone. If I show you, and teach you, and give you knowledge, you will keep it forever!"

Great teachers have the priceless ability to pass on lasting knowledge and encourage creative development. Ultimately, it's not the politicians and lawyers who will save this planet, as much as they'd like you to believe the contrary. I believe that the true fate of mankind lies in the sensibilities and skills of its teachers, be they school professors, private instructors, or parents.

If you have ever watched a young child discover his shadow for the first time, or the feel of sand, or the flight of a bird, you've seen a face filled with wonderment, excitement, and pure joy. That experience is the true gift of learning, for the teacher as well as the student. I offer this work as a celebration of that process and of the teachers who inspire us to grow and develop.

FLASHES OF DESTINY

"FOR WANT OF A NAIL...
THE KINGDOM WAS LOST."
— FROM AN OLD ENGLISH PROVERB

THE GREATEST WARRIOR IN THE GOLDEN AGE of the greatest kingdom in history rides his mighty stallion, confidently leading an undefeated army into yet another battle for Truth, Justice, and the Kingdom Way. Proudly, the steed rears up on its hind legs, elevating the warrior high above the troops to shout his battle cry. At that moment, unbeknownst to our robust duo, a loose nail falls from the stallion's shoe. As our powerful pair leads the charge and fervently gallops into the fray, the shoe is dislodged, causing the animal to stumble. Before the warrior can react, he is thrown. The massive horse trips and falls, crushing our hero. The tragedy sends instant panic through the troops. Confusion causes chaos. The battle is lost. The kingdom is vanquished.

And you thought this was going to be an uplifting book.

It gets better, I promise.

This little medieval ditty is a favorite of mine because it's a reminder that nothing should be taken for granted, and every moment in life is significant. It might seem that one's existence is nothing more than a long string of trivial details connected by a few planned milestones along the way. But one can never really be sure or even aware of when, where, how, or why the truly defining moments will occur—those pivotal points in time when a sudden cognition, an innocent decision, or acting upon a wild notion, will change the course of a person's life or establish his future's path.

The world's recorded history spins itself around such events. By chance, the young Galileo overheard a geometry lesson, awakening his interest in math. Darwin was inspired by a book he read just before his voyage on *HMS Beagle*. Einstein told of a dream that led him to the theory of relativity, and Gutenberg's idea for the printing press came to him in a sudden vision.

Then there are the tales—folklore wrapped around kernels of truth. I've always loved the story of the Greek scientist, Archimedes, becoming so excited after discovering his displacement principle (by sitting in a tub of water) that he jumped out of the bath and ran naked through the streets yelling "Eureka!" Or Newton's inspiration for his gravitation principles being sparked by watching the fall of an apple. Come to think of it, the apple has caused quite a stir over the years. Think how different the lives of Adam, William Tell, Johnny Appleseed, Snow White, and Mott would have been without it!

In retrospect, my captivation with fascinating communicators, the drive to discover the dynamics that make communication so powerful, and the satisfaction of helping individuals develop those elements, found their inspiration when I was five years old. I remember being alone in my room, intensely focused on a floor battle created with miniature plastic army figures, when I was suddenly struck by a captivating voice. Like a child following the Pied Piper of Hamelin, I dropped my handful of little green soldiers and slowly walked toward the engaging tones. In the kitchen, Mom was listening to an impassioned speaker on television while she fixed dinner. I found myself transfixed in front of that little black-and-white RCA, as a man filled the screen, and the room, with a charismatic vision:

I have a dream. . . . When we let freedom ring, when we let it ring from every state and every city, we will be able to speed up that day when all of God's children, black men and white men, Jews and Gentiles, Protestants and Catholics, will be able to join hands and sing, in the words of the Negro spiritual, "Free at last! Free at last! Thank God Almighty, we are free at last!"

All at once I was agitated, happy, sad, and mad. It made me want to do something. For the life of me, I didn't know what. But *something*! His emotions impacted on my soul. I was too young to fully understand the implications of his message. All I knew is that I was captivated. His energy actually came through the screen and clutched my heart. And I yearned to wield that same power. How did he do it?! I must have stormed around the house for a week after that day, bellowing and flailing, trying to captivate as he had captivated me. And, though the initial passion for making speeches subsided over time, my captivation for the art was now seared into my being forever.

To this day, when I see clips of Martin Luther King, Junior's speech at the 1963 civil rights march on Washington, D.C., I still feel those pangs of exhilaration. That speech and its delivery are a touchstone. King was a phenomenal communicator whose spirit still resonates today.

No one makes the decision to embark on a lifelong career as a "Fascinating Communicator." No university offers "Engaging Elocution" as a major. I would venture to guess that no parents have ever suggested to their children that if they eat right, work hard, and fight for truth, justice and the "Kingdom Way," they too could someday change the hearts of mankind through oratory. Communication is, however, intrinsic to the fabric of the many professions that guide, mold, and change our planet. The success of politicians, artists, religious leaders and myriad other public figures depends largely on their ability to affect individuals and groups through communication. It really doesn't matter how these communicators feel or what they believe: their life's blood, their survival, depends on what they can make others feel and believe.

Over the years, I have had the pleasure of working with, teaching, and getting to know many wonderfully talented communicators: actors, writers, newscasters, directors, producers, talk show hosts, religious leaders, and artists. Some were at the beginning of their careers, some at the top of their profession. A few have even allowed me to travel with them as coach, consultant, or confidant, on the long journey from struggling novice to "overnight success." In every case, I've observed common threads among those who became masters of their craft—underlying ideals, beliefs, points of view, and approaches to their respective areas of expertise—that are almost interchangeable in nature.

The following chapters include confessions given to me by a few of these masters who have enjoyed high levels of success in their particular fields and are strongly opinionated regarding their expertise. These discussions illuminate their successful facets, and complement the illustrations, tools and techniques set forth in this book, which can be used to acquire your own level of expertise. It is interesting to note that these masters don't always agree with one another, or even with the views expressed in this book. But discovering diverse points of view will help crystallize your understanding, opinions, and resolve, on your own journey toward mastery.

The cornerstones of my teaching have always been to enhance the people I work with as individuals, to nurture their unique personalities, and to cultivate intelligence and risk-taking within their craft. My goals are to promote personal style—a stamp that sets one apart—and the ability to be self-sufficient as a professional and as a person. This book is built on those same cornerstones, and dedicated to the art of fascinating communication.

IT'S NOT
WHAT YOU SAY

MASTER THE ART
OF POWERFUL
COMMUNICATION

Black-Belt Communicators

"The trick in our world is to make it
look easy . . . to make it look natural."
— Dick Clark

It's always a bit unsettling to see an anchor cry during a coaching session. Even though anchors and reporters usually take the frank conversations about their work to heart, they are usually fairly objective concerning the matter. Objectivity is, after all, something they've been trained for. On the other hand, a coach must sometimes delve into personal matters when the communicator needs to break free of a psychological problem restricting his or her further growth and development.

For example, an anchor I recently worked with happened to be amiable, witty, and full of charm in person, but on the air she was stiff and pedantic. Her presentation and delivery had energy but no life. As I broached the subject, her first reaction was defensive. As we got into it, I found that it was her issues with family and friends that caused her detachment on the air. Apparently, when she began her career, these "supportive" people in her life didn't believe she had it in her to be a serious journalist. Their collective "wisdom" convinced her that she was much too pretty, much too blond, and certainly not smart enough. To combat this criticism, she ran as far away from herself as possible. She dyed her hair and wore drab colors, and, over time, her on-air performance became a reflection of what she thought the ideal anchor was supposed to look and sound like. What started out as an exciting career that seemed to fit her spirited sensibilities and talents became an arduous daily task of pleasing others whom she secretly resented.

As she recounted her story and came to this realization, emotion welled and her tears began to flow. At that moment, while she wept, I asked her to read a news story from the scripts in front of her. What happened next was wonderful: With her defenses down and no one to please but herself, she read to me with her own voice, her own inflections, her own facial expressions and her own emotions. For the first time in a long time she was actually telling someone a story. And actually enjoying it. And her delivery was fascinating.

Since then she has moved to a bigger station in a bigger market and is doing beautifully. Recently, she sent me a videotape of a recent newscast, along with a note, which read:

> *Dear Bill,*
> *I wanted you to see the real me really telling stories. It's so much easier when you believe in yourself!*
> *Who knew hard news could be so much fun?*
> *Sincerely,*
> *(the real) Jennifer*

Dick Clark and the Lion

As "Jennifer" realized, to begin that first step down the path toward mastery, a person must first embrace the concept that at the core of every being lies an integrity and truth, and that honesty is one of the most powerful tools a communicator can wield. The person who can tap into those elements and consistently use them as a foundation for his craft is a formidable communicator indeed.

One such master, and a prime example of this philosophy in action, is Dick Clark. A major force in bringing rock-and-roll to television in the 1950s as host of *American Bandstand*, Mr. Clark's unpretentious and approachable style has bridged generation gaps for forty years, making his name synonymous with the notion of perpetual youth. Recently, we had a conversation in which Mr. Clark expressed his personal convictions on the subject of fascinating communication:

Dick Clark: I learned a long time ago that if you are going to reach the other person you must treat him as an ordinary human being, whether he is terribly wealthy or a criminal or a famous person. Whatever he is wrapped in doesn't mean anything once you get past the outer layer of the person.

I learned that as a twenty-seven year old kid in television. At one of the networks, I had a rather sadistic boss who seated me next to Henry J. Kaiser (one of the wealthiest men in the world) at a dinner party. I was sure he had seated me there just to see what the hell would happen to me because *Bandstand* was very hot. And Mr. Kaiser and I had very little in common.

We sat down next to one another at this formal dinner; I'm a rock-and-roll disk jockey for a television show with kids dancing, and here he was a financial kingpin. We didn't have a great deal to talk about. Then I noticed that he kept picking at his thumb. I said to him, "Mr. Kaiser, what seems to be the problem with your thumb?"

He said, "Oh, this damn thing. I got slivers in it while I was doing things around the house."

I asked if I could take a look at it. I always carry a small Swiss Army pocketknife that has all kinds of little doodads on it. I asked him if he would mind if I took a shot at his thumb. He said that he didn't mind and to go ahead. I took the little knife and got the sliver out. After that it was "Androcles and the Lion." We were the best of buddies the rest of the night.

You would do that for a four-year old. You would do it for an ancient person. You would do it for your mother, your dad, or an aunt or uncle. He appreciated it because he was usually treated all the time as if he was untouchable. So we had a great night!

So at the heart of it, Mr. Clark tells us that a good communicator touches a responsive chord in what people are interested in. He reaches out to them *as a real person* so that they will listen and communicate back to him in the same fashion.

Dick Clark: Years ago when I was an ugly, skinny, pimple-ridden and introverted teenager, my mother taught me this lesson: "It doesn't matter what you look like. People don't judge you by what you appear to be or your outward self. They want to know how you think about them as people. Always turn it over to the other person and you will always be in a winning position.

And how does that translate in the world of television's most famous show host?

Dick Clark: The trick in our world is to make it look easy. To make it look natural. Regardless of the most pressure filled or hurried or god-awful situation you may find yourself in, you want that audience to say to themselves, "Nothing will go wrong here. Good ol' Bob or Dick or whoever is going to get me through this. I'm in good hands." That must be part of the host's communicative abilities.

Faux-Belt Masters

Every year, thousands of Americans across the country go through "testings" in Karate dojos, to receive colored belt upgrades. Each colored belt signifies a proficiency level, with the Black Belt and all its degrees representing the best or highest rank one can obtain. Seemingly, once martial arts students have hit black belt status, they have reached the high end of the line: Nirvana; Masters of the Universe.

This system seems fairly logical, right? I once asked a Korean Tae Kwon Do sensei why the colored belt system was not consistent in all dojos. Why, in fact, any one color might very well represent a different level of proficiency, depending on the dojo or the martial arts discipline one belongs to. I inquired, "Isn't that confusing? Doesn't Korea put out some kind of official colored belt reference book?" (Korea is where many of the martial arts, such as Tae Kwon Do, originated.) "I mean, how am I supposed to tell who I can beat up and who I should avoid at parties?"

Well, the sensei just smiled wryly and whispered into my ear, "The only thing we use colored belts for in Korea is to hold up our pants." He went on to explain that, just as Italian pizza was really perfected right here in the good ol' USA, the martial arts colored belt hoopla is actually a Western ritual, created to satisfy Americans' need to validate their accomplishments. Eastern cultures look at self-development as a life-long process. And a true master, in any field, knows that mastery is a journey, not a destination.

In this country however, the *MTV* attitude, "I want it fast and I want it now," has been indelibly printed on our collective DNA. Never mind quality. The ability to acquire quickly and the need to then "show and tell" has become a measure of our self-worth. Dick Clark encapsulates this cultural phenomenon by comparing his *Bandstand* audience with today's television viewers:

Dick Clark: Forty years ago when *Bandstand* first started, it was a musical film show that quickly evolved into human beings live in front of the camera, which was a little more fun. By the time we reached the end of the line, television changed. The mind-set and the attention span of the average young viewer had shrunk to a few moments. You can't put on an hour and a half of kids dancing to records and hope to maintain their interest any longer. Our time came and went.

Today we do everything with the idea that we have got to hold on to them or that we had better promise them something in ten minutes from now so that they will at least stay with us for awhile. It is a frightening social disease we've given everybody. We don't dwell on things very long anymore.

This national compulsion for instant gratification isn't focused ex-clusively on television. It has permeated our way of life, driving us to substitute fast-food fare for four-star Epicurean delights, replace in-depth news reporting with pithy sound-bites, manufacture frivolous lawsuits faster than bees regurgitate honey, and, in our society's inter-course, supplant the world's greatest literature with T-shirt maxims such as "He Who Dies With The Most Toys Wins" and "I'm With Stu-pid." This "social disease" has turned the idea of mastery as a lifelong journey into a colored belt that can be won in the nearest dojo.

The second step down the path toward mastery is the real understanding that instant gratification, however enjoyable, is ultimately fleeting. Masters in all fields know that as they succeed in their daily endeavors, there must also be an ongoing process of development and preparation to maintain consistency of quality and style in their work.

Dick Clark: Part of the problem with some talk shows is that people don't prepare enough. Right now there is a well-known, very successful talker who prides himself on not preparing. Anybody who wants to be critical would say that he would have been a lot better off if he had read the damn book.

For Golden Globe Awards shows, I interview the winners backstage. Say there were eighty possible winners. Then there were eighty personalities that I had notes on. I read all their biographies and I had seen all the primary nominated shows that I thought I would have to deal with. So I knew what their work was. That takes a few weeks of preparation.

You come over-prepared in case they are going to run dry. You don't want to be staring and ask, "And where do you go next?" That is the worst thing you can ask anybody. Or, "Did you like the show?" Those are fallback questions that desperate amateurs use. Usually, listening to what they had to say right before we went on the air, or during the course of the on-air conversation, leads you off in a whole different direction that you never thought you were going to get to. Which brings us to something else about good communication: always listen!

So preparation is key in the process a great communicator uses, which allows the audience access to his integrity and truth. Preparation strengthens consistency of quality and style as well as the communicator's ability to listen. Any preparation requires an investment of time. The Master's preparation is a lifelong process of learning and practice.

BAROMETERS

Most professionals can point to tangible manifestations of their talents. Scientists have formulas, theorems, and inventions as measures of achievement. The architect's genius is evidenced by his creation of beautiful and timeless structures. The gourmet chef produces four-star meals, award-winning desserts, and holiday cookbooks. Mechanics, farmers, builders, and plumbers can all point to concrete evidence of their success. But what does the communicator have as a barometer of self-worth? In terms of success or failure, professional communicators can only point to themselves. Their canvas is face and body; their product emanates directly from the soul.

In the first session with a new student, an accomplished teacher or coach will usually inquire as to the results that person wants from the process. Invariably, whether the tutee is an actor, anchor, politician, etc., the tutor finds the reply as bland as milquetoast, usually along the lines of "I just want to be better." When pressed for specifics, many first-time clients have difficulty articulating a desired final product. Because the mercury of a communicator's barometer is visceral, his goals are seldom tangible, and the description of his needs is often psychological. Here are the top five responses I've heard over the years, when asking first-time clients what results they would like to gain from the sessions:

"What I'm doing sometimes feels phony."

"I would really like it to come more naturally."

"I don't want to feel like I'm manufacturing the emotions."

"I want to be myself and feel that what I have to offer is enough."

"How can I be convincing about a subject I couldn't care less about?!"

For most, it really boils down to three things. Professional communicators who take a vested interest in their craft want:

- To know that they are continually improving

- To know that they hit the mark with some kind of consistency

- To feel that they are in control

Simple. Not unlike Rubik's Cube. You know there's a solution. You've seen it done. All it takes is focus, persistence and lifelong commitment. Like I said, simple.

Later, we will explore various tools and techniques Master Communicators have discovered and used to succeed and win on a consistent basis. But first, let's take a little quiz.

If you are interested in becoming a better communicator, or just fascinated by the process, this series of questions should stimulate your curiosity and start you on the road to mastery. But don't over-analyze. Just take out a sheet of paper and quickly jot down a best guess for each question. Use your answer sheet as a bookmark to easily check yourself against the right answers as they reveal themselves throughout this book. (Don't you just hate that?! If it's really going to drive you crazy, the answers may be found in Chapter 10.) I would suggest, however, that you discover the solutions gradually, as you read. Doing so will allow for a better understanding of the reasoning that supports each answer. It will also increase your retention and strengthen your ability to utilize the information. Besides, I dare you not to look ahead!

THE QUIZ

1. "I never said I thought you were crazy."
This sentence has a definite element of
    a. Humor   b. Doubt
    c. Anger   d. All of the above
    e. Impossible to tell

2. The most powerful element of communication is —
    a. Visual   b. Audible
    c. Emotional   d. Sexual   e. Textual

3. "I love you."
This sentence can be verbalized how many different ways?
    a. Three   b. Nine
    c. No more than thirty d. At least fifty

4. Energy equals—
    a. Liveliness, animation, and vivacity
    b. Bigger, louder, and faster
    c. Investment
    d. mc^2

5. What percentage of a person's communication comprehension is tonal? What percentage is textual? What percentage is visual?

6. Marie Curie—
    a. Raised two daughters
    b. Raised a daughter who became an accomplished musician
    c. Raised a daughter who won a Nobel Prize
    d. Became the first person ever to win two Nobel Prizes
    e. All of the above
    f. a & d

7. Who coined the phrase, "Float like a butterfly, sting like a bee!"?
   a Dennis Rodman   b. Mike Tyson
   c. Michael Jordan   d. Muhammad Ali

8. History's milestones —
   a. Are stamped with the speeches of
      fascinating communicators
   b. Weigh heavy on our country's leaders
   c. Always seem to come in threes
   d. Are recorded by history's "winners"

9. Communicators are generally remembered for their —
   a. Talent   b. Body of work
   c. Quality   d. Maxims

10. Tertiary Core Characters are —
    a. The cast of *Baywatch*
    b. One-third of the Chinese language
    c. The bulk of Master Communicators
    d. Personalities experienced over the course of a lifetime

11. The brain retains concepts by —
    a. Electrical processing
    b. Synapse activity
    c. Storing hard data
    d. Attaching pictures and emotions

12. The eyes are —
    a. A good indicator of truth
    b. The "windows to the soul"
    c. Involuntary reactors
    d. All of the above

13. The audience/viewers are always effected by —
    a. The human condition   b. Text
    c. Subtext   d. Characterizations

14. Intention is —
    a. A key element in learning
    b. A key element when questioning authority
    c. A key element in success
    d. a & c
    e. All of the above

15. The "Stanislavski Three" represent —
    a. A Russian mime troupe
    b. Questions the actor should answer
       regarding his own existence
    c. The owners of the Moscow Art Theatre
    d. Questions the actor should answer
       regarding a character's existence

16. "Ceiling values" poses the questions —
    a. "How much?" and "How pressing?"
    b. "Who?" "What?" "Where?" "When?" "How?" and "Why?"
    c. "How bad?" and "Who cares?"
    d. "How many lines do I have?" and "How much in residuals will
       I make?"

17. In 1997, Troy Aikman took on a specialized coach for —
    a. His golf game
    b. Basic quarterback skills
    c. Ballet
    d. Line dancing

18. Uncontrollable tail wagging in cats signifies —
    a. An overdose of catnip
    b. Acute conflict
    c. A kittygasm
    d. A feline with an attitude

19. Eighty-two percent of TV viewers think reporters are —
    a. The driving force of any newscast
    b. Their pipeline to the most immediate information
    c. Insensitive to people's pain
    d. "Wannabe" anchors

20. It is possible to be unbiased *and* —
    a. Give your opinion
    b. Be a great partner
    c. Be a national spokesman for a product
    d. Convey the human condition

THE RATS, THE PACK, AND THE MASTERS

Before learning the tools and techniques of great communication, it is important to know exactly what we're shooting for. The more you know about your destination, the better prepared you'll be when you arrive. After all, it's rather difficult to hit a target unless you can see it clearly. So, to begin crystallizing our goals, let's start with what constitutes a remarkable communicator.

Career communicators, who are seemingly in it for the long haul, can be divided into three groups, which I call **The Rats, The Pack and The Masters.**

The Rats are those faux-communicators who really don't belong in the business. They have no technique, no control and no real respect for the craft. They aren't sure what they're doing, not sure how they got there, and not sure where they're going. They are the ones who spawned the phrases, "wouldn't know the truth if it bit him in the face" and "couldn't relate her way out of a paper bag." Unfortunately, the combination of bad TV, 'B' movies and cable access has given us a plethora of these personalities. They are the ones you watch with an incredulous expression as you think to yourself, "Is there no justice on this planet?!" Like rats on a ship, they're difficult to eradicate. Not much can be done to rectify the situation, except kick them away when they get too close.

The Pack is the largest segment of communicators. They are a respectable lot and, for the most part, perform their craft adequately. Although, in terms of success, some may be at the front of the pack and some at the rear, they all seem to be conscientious, have energy, and are interesting to the average viewer. There is really nothing wrong with belonging to this group. Their product is accepted as the "norm" and they do seem to get their message across. That message, however, is oftentimes mediocre. We've experienced it hundreds of times before with slight variations. And like the background music played in elevators and department stores, after a time, it all tends to sound the same.

Communicate: To make known; Impart. To have an interchange, as of thoughts or ideas. To be connected or form a connecting passage.[1]

Looking at the dictionary definition of "communicate," we find that it fits *The Pack* because it, too, is adequate and pedestrian in nature. It really doesn't give you a feel for the subject. When I ponder communication, I think of that old Memorex commercial where the opera singer hits so high a note that a wineglass bursts. The image serves to remind me that communication, especially the voice, is actually tangible. It has mass and the capability to impinge on another object or affect the listener. When you consider the implications of communication as a substantive instrument, the ability to control and utilize it effectively can be extremely powerful. In a world full of distractions, the fascinating communicator can command a person's or a group's attention, manipulate emotions, even change the course of thoughts, views, or ideas. And, like splitting the atom, the force of communication can be used to create—or destroy.

The Masters can then be characterized as those fascinating communicators who control and effectively use communication as a means to impart thoughts, ideas, and feelings in such a way as to physically and emotionally move those receiving their message. Masters are not satisfied with the mundane job of delivering data, but constantly strive to find new ways of making their communication fresh, fervent, and alive. A Master's ultimate goal is to constantly deliver communication that comes wrapped within the core quality of his or her being.

Finding the best path that leads toward mastery requires a clear understanding of the final destination. To begin this process, it is important to realize how other successful communicators developed and honed their crafts—not only those who practice your specific area of interest and not only those in present time; it is important to have an overview of the Masters throughout history.

> *Dick Clark:* For anyone wanting to begin a career as a communicator, I would say to watch all the people who do it, and do what the good ones do, and don't do what the bad ones do. Simple.

Now that we have a general description of the Master Communicator, the next chapter will take a look at specific examples of a few past masters in order to solidify our own objectives for the future.

QUALITY KEYS

- *The barometer of self-worth*: Family and friends are not always the best source of validation for the professional communicator. Success or failure can be measured only by what the communicator personally has to offer. His canvas is face and body; his product emanates directly from the soul.

- *Believe in yourself!* To be yourself you must believe in yourself. To utilize your natural talents, you must trust that they are valid.

- *Coaching the professional communicator*: Communicators who take a vested interest in their craft usually want three basic results from their coaching sessions:

  To improve
  To gain control
  To hit the mark with consistency

- *Goals*: The more you know about your destination, the better prepared you'll be when you arrive. After all, it's rather difficult to hit a target unless you can see it clearly.

- *The Rats*: Those faux-communicators who have no technique, no control, and no real respect for the craft.

- *The Pack*: Communicators who perform their craft adequately. Their product is generally accepted as the "norm," although their delivery is sometimes mediocre and oftentimes pedestrian.

- *The Masters*: Those fascinating communicators who control and effectively use communication as a means of imparting thoughts, ideas, and feelings in such a way as to physically and emotionally move those receiving their message.

2 INTENTION

ALL RIGHT, LET'S TAKE A LOOK AT THE TOP TWENTY reasons why you will
never become a great communicator:

"I just don't have the time."

"I'm not attractive enough."

"My intelligence intimidates people."

"I'm too short."

"You can't teach an old dog new tricks!"

"I have a speech impediment."

"I don't want to be somebody else. I like me just the way I am."

"I'm too heavy."

"I was taught to speak well, which really intimidates people."

"It could never happen to me. I never win at anything."

"People don't take me seriously because I'm too attractive."

"I don't have the money."

"My height intimidates people."

"I'm not really that bright."

"I'm too shy."

"I have children to raise and a house to attend to."

"I'm so thin, people don't give any weight to what I have to say."

"I'm just very intimidated by people."

"You're confusing me with someone who has talent."
"I'm just too stupid, fat, and ugly."

What? You say you would never utter such nonsense? You say you feel you've just been insulted? Or is it just the opposite? Maybe a few of these remarks hit too close to home.

Take another look. Are they all really so outlandish? Maybe you have never actually defended yourself with one of these statements to another person, but what of the "inner critic?" You know the creature I'm talking about—that monster inside your head that constantly reminds you of your faults and shortcomings. The "self-talk" that automatically clicks on before each decision is made, suggesting you take the safest out, avoiding any chance of failure.

Well, believe it or not, the above "top twenty reasons" are exact quotes from clients/students I have worked with over the years. Similar types of rationalizations are given all the time as explanations for **The Pack** member's pedestrian lot in life. They are rationales explaining **The Pack's** inability to attain "black belt" status, justifications for being dilettantes. Stymied by these insurmountable obstacles standing between themselves and their talents; many seek a "quick fix." Sadly, for some that literally translates into taking drugs. For others it means seeking professional counsel. Their hope, of course, is to find that special person, be it priest, psychiatrist or guru, who can whisk away all foibles with the wave of a magic wand. The few communicators in **The Pack** who are smart enough to embrace the "mastery is a journey" concept will find a consultant/teacher/coach who'll invest time and energy in showing them how to live successfully with that inner critic. It is a part of being human, and there is no easy or practical way to make it simply disappear.

When a communicator seeks help in this area, the teacher should make sure that the coaching process includes the study of a few great achievers from history. He should arbitrarily choose and summarily review the lives of several men and women whose accomplishments were pivotal in the course of human development, and whose creations, ideas, or speeches moved the hearts and minds of millions. On the surface, marveling at those seemingly superhuman feats makes one feel puny by contrast. On closer inspection, however, there is a startling realization that these "extraordinary" individuals were just as fragile, just as hampered by life's injustices, and just as human as the rest of humankind. It's sometimes easier to deal with and overcome one's personal fears and frustrations when seeing them in the context of those success stories.

Take, for example, Ludwig van Beethoven. The first signs of hearing loss appeared in his late twenties—not a good thing for a musician—yet he continued to compose beautiful music. Beethoven became completely deaf in his late forties. It was after this point in his life that he composed his greatest masterpieces.

Muhammad didn't begin his teachings until he was forty years old, yet he founded one of the world's major religions, and became ruler of Arabia.

Albert Einstein did poorly in high school math, and had to work in a patent office to make ends meet. Adding insult to injury, Einstein met with mountains of controversy when proposing the theories that would eventually revolutionize science—and the world.

Marie Curie brought up two extraordinary daughters. One daughter became an accomplished musician and author. The other daughter won a Nobel Prize. This in itself, as any mother will tell you, is quite a life's accomplishment. It is even more amazing when you consider that, while raising those two daughters, Madame Curie herself became the first person ever to win two Nobel Prizes.

How easy it would have been for any of these individuals to give up their dreams when faced with adversity and accept the cards fate dealt them as insurmountable hurdles. Instead, they chose to persevere. And in the end isn't that what defines the very essence of a winner? Is it not the decisions one makes when faced with seemingly impossible obstacles? The willingness to continue on the path toward resolution and success, though it may take a lifetime?

Why is it that most people are satisfied to run with **The Pack**, willing to accept mediocrity as a fact of life? And what is it that separates them from **The Masters**, those individuals who seem to succeed on a consistent basis? What is the through-line that connects all winners in all areas of expertise? What is the essence of a winner?

ESSENCE OF A WINNER

Ronnie Clemmer is a United Press International Award-winning producer and three-time Emmy nominee. He has had successful careers as a reporter and producer in broadcast news (featured on such national venues as ESPN, CNN, CBS, and ABC's *Nightline*) and as an executive producer in the entertainment industry. His producing credits include Columbia Pictures' box office smash *A League of Their Own*, starring Tom Hanks, Geena Davis and Madonna, and HBO's Silver Hugo Award-winning *A Private Matter*, starring Sissy Spacek and Aidan Quinn. Mr. Clemmer's personal achievements, coupled with the experience of working with so many successful individuals in both sports and entertainment, have given him unique insight into the winner's character and nature.

Ronnie Clemmer: The one thing they have in common is focus. An ability at any given point to understand that the task is all, to focus on it with a calmness and with an intensity that makes others around them know that they are seriously in the zone of doing what they do. It is that distractibility that so often trips up performers and athletes. The guys who have always had the greatest game effort, who had the 300-yard gain, who scored the fifty-six points in a basketball game, who won two Olympic gold medals, are the guys who, at a certain point, hear less of everything around them and see less of everything around them. Time slows down and they see the particles of time of the event that they are actually focused on. They are able to focus on each individual second of their performance. They don't stay outside of themselves, wondering what others are thinking about or thinking, "How am I doing? or "If I fail at this, then what will I do?" The ability to push all that aside and focus on nothing but the task at hand separates champions from also-rans in every profession I've ever known.

I'll never forget something that boxer Ken Norton said to me about a month before he was to defend his title as heavyweight champion of the world. I got to know Mr. Norton in the early 1980s, while he was exploring the possibilities of an acting career. "Kenny" was just about the nicest guy in the world. Which is why it always amazed me that he was so talented at beating the living daylights out of people.

One day I asked Kenny, "What is the hardest aspect of winning?"

I assumed he would talk about the grueling hours of training or the physical stress inherent in each bout. What he actually told me was much more fascinating than anything I had imagined.

Kenny thought for a long moment and answered, "The hardest thing about winning? Everyone expects me to do it again!"

How about that for a justification? Not only does winning take concerted effort and is difficult to achieve, but once you win, you're expected to keep winning! It would be so much easier not to win; to remain the victim of circumstance. And what if you attempt to grab that brass ring and fail? How do you live with yourself then?

Then I asked Kenny, "So why keep winning?"

His expression suddenly changed. He looked down at me (Kenny's a big guy), his eyes sparkled and his smile beamed wide and boyish.

"It's what I do!" he said.

Ronnie Clemmer: Almost all skills that separate winners from also-rans are innate skills to some extent. They already have them and then they perfect them. For those of us who are not so perfectly created out of the womb, the ability to perceive those skills, analyze what they are, and learn them is what makes us better champions in our life. What Michael Johnson teaches about running, everybody can learn from. It won't make any of us a 400-meter champion in the Olympics, but we can still learn from him and apply those things to everything we do in our daily lives.

Everyone has problems. Everyone has good reasons for not attempting improvements, good reasons to avoid crawling out on that limb. But those "success stories"—the winners and achievers among us—are no different from anyone else. What sets them apart is their choice to ignore the naysayers; their resolve to play against the odds; their decision to act like winners, to think like winners, and to feel like winners. Their belief that they deserve to be and in fact are winners. Even though a specific trophy might be nowhere in sight.

EXERCISE # 1 :

(You will need paper and pencil for this.)

Think about something you've been wanting to accomplish but keep putting off. It could be as simple as joining a gym or as involved as building a house. What are the hurdles standing in the way of your starting the project? What are the hurdles standing in the way of your success?

Now, take out a blank sheet of paper and write down the goal and next to it write down the three biggest reasons why you haven't done anything about it. And be honest. Intangible reasons like "My friends would find the idea stupid" are just as valid (and just as important to note) as tangible reasons like "Not enough time." Here's an example:

GOAL	HURDLES
Find a better job.	I don't have the time to look.
	I'm not qualified to do anything else.
	I don't have a resume.
	I'm ashamed to ask anyone for help.
	If Mom found out, she'd have a conniption fit.
	Etc.

In writing down your goal and hurdles, you might have already come to the conclusion that procrastination is no longer necessary. In either case, read on. We'll refer back to this exercise later.

Exam Cram

During the early 1970s, academic research was done to determine the amount of information that alumni actually retain one year after graduation. It was concluded that, on average, students are only able to speak intelligently about 19 percent of the material they studied during their undergraduate programs. Now, I'm no Rhodes scholar, but I make that out to be about nine productive months out of four years of schooling. Ouch! How does that happen? Is the American student's attention span that short? Aren't they eating a good breakfast every morning? At the current cost of education, it sounds as if each student is flushing away at least $60,000.

To unravel that enigma, consider this scenario: A student skates through a whole semester of a particularly boring class, only to be gripped by the fearful realization that the final exam is *tomorrow*! Now, up to this point he hasn't made the slightest effort to learn a thing, and if he doesn't do some major cramming tonight, he'll fail miserably in the morning. So, to keep from becoming the world's oldest living freshman, our egghead spends the entire night cramming every piece of information he can possibly fit into the little part of his brain that actually cares about the subject. And lo and behold, the next day he takes that test and *passes it*! Ha!

But wait. What happens after the exam? Does the student remember what he studied? If he had to take the same test again the following week, would he retain all the information he so diligently stuffed into his cranium? And do as well? The most likely answer to both questions is "No!"

The reason most students don't retain information they learn specifically for a test is quite simple. It is because they learn that information *specifically for a test*. They program their brain to understand that the information that is being hammered into it is for a specific, short-term purpose only, so the data is stored in short-term memory. (Short-term memory is sort of like the "garage-sale items" section of the brain, for items we couldn't possibly want or use, so we store them for a brief time, knowing we'll "pawn them off" as soon as possible!) When the exam is over, the brain dumps those items from short-term memory, making way for the next pile of "useless" information. It was discovered that students memorize about 80 percent of their school subjects with the sole *intention* of passing tests, and by so doing, end up retaining only about 20 percent of the material given to them in school.

INTENTION IS KEY

Intention is a key element in learning. If your intention in study is to do nothing more than pass tests, much of your time is being wasted on that endeavor. If, however, your intention is to learn the material for practical application in your career or in day-to-day living, it is likely you'll retain much more of that information and have a greater comprehension and appreciation of that subject. The same can be said for reading books or watching presentations. If, for instance, you read a biography out of curiosity, you might or might not find it enjoyable. If, on the other hand, your intention is to invest yourself in the reading, you might keep a dictionary on hand to look up unfamiliar words and phrases. You might also discuss various elements with a friend. In so doing, your comprehension and enjoyment of the material will definitely be enhanced.

Intention is also a key element in success. Successful individuals—those who continually make great strides in their personal and/or professional lives—seem to do so by setting short-term and long-term goals with target dates to complete those goals. For them, creating these *intentions* to follow is the best recipe for consistent, long-lasting achievements.

Patrick Swayze is one of the best examples of success-through-intentions. I first got to know Patrick about sixteen years ago. At that time, he had already been successful as a gymnast touring North and Central America with *Disney on Parade*, as a principal ballet dancer with the Elliot Feld Ballet in New York, as a Broadway star in the lead role of Danny Zuko in *Grease*, and as a film actor in *Skatetown, USA*. And in all the years since, he has never lost his dedication, fervency, and love for the craft of acting. He has twice been nominated for a Golden Globe Award, has worked with some of the best directors in Hollywood, such as Roland Joffe, Jerry Zucker and Francis Ford Coppola, and has starred in such blockbusters as *The Outsiders*, *Dirty Dancing*, and *Ghost*. I have always found Patrick's intentions to be extremely focused and crystal clear. I recently asked him about those intentions in terms of his career:

Patrick Swayze: I've redefined my goals in the last few years. Okay, here's the movie star. I've been around a long time. So, what else is there? For a while it messed with my head because it almost destroyed my dreams. It almost destroyed my passion because this is as far as my goals went. The idea was to be a big star. The best way to screw up someone's life is to give them what they want. Then I found that the real key to life is passion. The key to life is the process, not the goal.

I came to that realization by getting into Eastern philosophies years ago. *Zen and the Art of Archery, Zen and the Art of Motorcycle Maintenance.* The idea of shooting an arrow with a spiritual goal, not toward a target. Allowing your spirit, allowing your soul, allowing some little bird inside of you telling you when it's perfect to release that arrow. Not your mind. Not even your skill. Because in tournament shooting, you never miss the bull's-eye. You're judged instead on how perfectly your arrows are formed in a cylinder coming straight out of the center of that bull's-eye. Yet, you're shooting straight up at a hundred meters. And that's when I thought, "There's something to this stuff!" And I realized that there's power inside of us that we've never even imagined.

Now, I take it much more on a physical level than on a metaphysical level. I want to feel it now. I want to do the metaphysical stuff to feel the physical. I want to see if people can truly, like Norman Cousins in his book, *Anatomy of an Illness*, totally cure themselves of cancer through laughter. Of course, there is the physical aspect, through the endocrine system, of stimulating the correct endorphins to battle. But the whole key is the power of intention. The greater your power of following through with an intention, the greater an actor you will become. Or the better director or the better grip or the better writer.

So what are your intentions? How are you supposed to create them? Where do you find the cookbook that outlines the recipes for your achievements? And how long is it going to take, anyway? Just like everyone else in our fast-paced, instant-gratification society, you want your wins now—*right now!*

There is a good news/bad news scenario when it comes to creating intentions. You might consider it bad news that no cookbook or roadmap exists to dictate where your specific intentions should lead you. It might also be a little aggravating to realize it's going to take a lot of time and mental work to come up with these intentions. How much time? That ball is also in your court. Time is relative in this situation. It depends a lot on the individual's innate abilities and resolve.

Now the good news: Creating intentions is free! No one can keep you from it and anyone can do it! (How many things in life can you say *that* about?) Although I can't tell you what you should consider as personal goals, I can give you a few hints on the "how-to" of creating intentions.

For starters, let's begin by taking a look at several definitions for the word *intention*:[2]

Intention: *Resolve. A determination to act in a certain way. What one intends to do or bring about. A concept considered as the product of attention directed to an object of knowledge.*

The description that really grabs me is the last one. If there was ever a blueprint for *intention*, this is it. Look at it again.

Intention: *A concept considered as the product of attention directed to an object of knowledge.*

This particular definition tells us that *intention* is not just a *desire* to do something. *Intention* implies directing creative energy toward something you *understand*. Seems pretty simple. To have an intention, you have to have *knowledge* of the object you are trying to achieve. And it only follows that the more knowledge you have concerning that object or goal, the stronger your *intention* will be. It almost sounds as if one must work backward to create an *intention*. Actually, that is exactly what it sounds like. And ultimately, it is exactly what should be done.

SHOOTING FOR THE MOON

As an example of working backward to obtain a goal, let's take a quick and whimsical look at mankind's first moon landing. As *intentions* go, the Apollo program was one of the grandest realized in this planet's history. When the National Aeronautics and Space Administration (NASA) was formed in the late 1950s, the good ol' boys in Houston didn't just look up at the moon and say, "Hey, let's build a rocket, shove in a couple guys, shoot it off and see how close we can get to that big white ball of feta cheese up there!" If that were the case, it might have taken fifty years of trial-and-error flights to finally reach their dream. Instead, they realized their goal within a relatively short time by asking and answering a bazillion questions before attempting it:

- How far is it?
- How big is it?
- How much gravitational pull?
- What toys will we want to take with us to play in our solar system's biggest sandbox?
- What souvenirs will we bring home?
- What kind of dune buggy works best on cheese?
- If three guys travel for three weeks consuming nothing but three hundred pounds of freeze-dried beef jerky and Tang, how much should be added to Apollo's budget for psychological counseling once our boys return home?
- Etc.

NASA formulated exactly what they wanted the final product of their intention to look like, and they worked backward from there. Once they decided what they wanted to do and what they would need to send with the astronauts to do it, then they could figure out how big the spaceship should be, and the exact number of glove compartments needed. Only after the architects came up with the blueprints for that baby could the engineers figure out exactly how they were going to get it off of the ground, how much fuel would be needed for a round trip, and so on.

Of course, the process NASA went through was much more technical and complicated than what I've just described, but you get the idea. The point is *knowledge*. The more one knows about the intention, the more one can visualize the final product, the greater chance for success, and the sooner that success will be realized.

Intention Spin-off

Often, the fear of failure keeps people from setting intentions. The justification for not establishing goals is that, in the end, if a goal were striven for and not achieved, the loss would be too devastating.

I submit to you that this line of thinking is in itself a great loss to the individual and his life's experience. In fact, it is contrary to our nature as human beings. Without the penchant of aiming for preset objectives, especially difficult or seemingly impossible objectives created out of the imagination, human history would have few grand achievements. There would be no wonderful architecture, no Industrial Revolution, no medical breakthroughs, no means of travel that would surpass riding horseback. In effect, the Stone Age would have actually been our Golden Age.

Let's forget grand achievements for a moment. There is another great benefit to setting and striving toward goals. It is called "*intention spin-off.*" This is the by-product of striving for a goal. For example, if you were to train for a year to run hurdles in the Olympics, you might not win the gold medal, but your intention spin-offs would probably be more powerful leg muscles, a stronger heart, and greater stamina.

To illustrate on a larger scale, imagine for a moment that NASA labored all those years and, at the last moment, failed to realize its goal. The whole intention was to visit the moon but, for whatever reason, the ship just couldn't land and had to return home. Well, it's been said the actual landing, as momentous as it was, did not compare to the scientific and medical discoveries made during the overall process of getting there. Stronger and lighter alloys, better computer technologies, and better nutritional supplements were all discovered as spin-offs of NASA's intention to land on the moon. Without the efforts to realize that intention, many other breakthroughs would not have taken place at that time in our history.

Therefore, to the Master Communicator, "What if I fail?" should have little significance or validity. In fact, the questions become, "What if I don't create an intention? What is the cost of not trying?" Without intentions there is no journey. Without a journey there is no learning, no growth and no development.

Having intentions and striving to attain goals can never be a losing proposition if one realizes the benefits inherent in the journey to obtain that goal.

EXERCISE #2:

(You will need paper and pencil for this.)

Below I have listed examples of a short-term and long-term intention, with target dates for completion.

Short-term Intention: *Haircut*
Target Date: *Saturday*
Long-term Intention: *Compete in 10k run*
Target date: *"This Summer"*

Now it's your turn. Take out a sheet of paper and list three short-term and three long-term intentions. It doesn't matter how important or trivial they are. What's important is that you sincerely believe these intentions must be accomplished. Next to each intention, come up with a target date and write it down.

DOWN TO EARTH

To bring this idea of *intention* closer to home, take a look at Sherri Allen's story. Sherri is a wonderfully gifted anchor who has been in broadcast news for over eighteen years and is currently the mainline female anchor at KTBS.[3] During a recent coaching session, as one of our discussions centered on her future *intentions*, Sherri told me an interesting story about her start in the business:

Sherri Allen: I don't know exactly what it is. I just decide I'm going to do something, find out what it is I have to accomplish to do that thing and just do it. I guess I've always been able to envision what I want. And when I envision it, if it seems too big for me, it becomes a challenge that makes me want to go after it even more.

Seeing the goal clearly is necessary to getting there. I remember while working on my masters at Northwestern State University, I would watch the local news in Shreveport and think, "You know, I can do that!" And, as time went on I thought, "That's what I want." And I could see that. It was so clear. And I knew that I could do it, but I had never been on television before, so I also knew that it would take a number of years. I have to have a dream or I don't have the passion.

It's interesting to note that this kind of story has been told countless times by successful individuals throughout history: Leonardo da Vinci, Jesse Owens, Pablo Picasso, Frank Lloyd Wright, and so many others. The events leading up to their achievements invariably would include a strong vision in the imagination, giving them passion to accomplish their goals.

Sherri Allen: At the time, I had a sales job with a statewide publication based in Natchitoches. One day, back in 1985, instead of going on sales calls, I jumped in the company car and drove over to KD Studios in Dallas.[4] I had done some modeling and thought I could go into television commercials as a start, so I met with the director of admissions there, Michal Berry. She looked at my portfolio and said, "You don't have it for TV commercials. But you do have a presence for television news." So she sent me to Sandra Connell, who was the head of talent placement at Audience Research and Development.[5] This was a Friday afternoon. Sandra sat me down, showed me example tapes of other anchors and said, "This is what you need to do." She showed me how they dressed and helped me to create my vision.

The very next Monday, I went to Shreveport and just knocked on the doors of all three stations. The CBS affiliate said, "We're between news directors so you'll have to come back next week. The ABC affiliate said, "We don't have any studio time for you to make a tape" (because I didn't have an example tape of my own) "so you'll have to come back next Wednesday when we'll have studio time." So I went to KTAL, the NBC affiliate, and they let me audition on the spot. The next day I called and they asked if I would be willing to go to Texarkana and get my feet wet reporting in television. And so I did. And I stayed in Texarkana for three months working sixteen-hour days learning how to report for television. Three months later KTAL brought me back to Shreveport and made me the mainline anchor.

I told Sherri that she made it sound too incredibly easy to just walk in off the street and get a job on television. Without missing a beat, she said:

Sherri Allen: Keep in mind that I was in sales. I knew how to market myself and I considered myself extremely professional. I just looked at it as a business and that I was marketing a product. I was there on a cold sales call and I was going to use everything I had learned to make the transition to television. And besides, I had a strong amount of confidence. It was all part of my vision.

And after Sherri's first month of being their mainline anchor, KTAL's ratings went from last place to first place for the first time in twenty years.

CORE APPLICATION

Sherri Allen's story is quite an example of achieving goals by having clear *intentions*! Now that we've talked about intentions on a grand scale and on an individual level, let's get personal. What about *your* intentions? Do you have a strong vision of your future? Do you have solid intentions regarding your career, your relationships, your life? No matter what style of communication your career is grounded in, be it entertainment, broadcast news, religion or politics, having clear intentions is a key factor of your success.

If your *intention* in reading this book is application, here's an assignment for you:

EXERCISE #3:

Decide who and what you will be in ten years.

Yes, I'm serious. Get out some paper, open up your laptop or turn on that home-PC and begin writing. And the statement, "I want to be rich and famous" doesn't count. It's too general, and therefore means nothing. *Rich* and *famous* are relative terms. Exactly how much money delineates *rich* to you? What does *famous* entail? How would it manifest itself? Your description of the future must be as exact and detailed as possible. Describe where you would like your career to be, detail all the facets of that career, in what part of the world you will reside, the nature of your personal relation-ships, your business relationships, your house(s), your car(s), your financial status, your skills, your pets, everything. Brainstorm. Don't allow the "inner critic" to curtail your imagination. Just because you only have $17 in your savings account at present doesn't mean you can't have $170,000 in ten years. People have done it with less, in less time. And don't be discouraged if you can't bang out this paper in fifteen minutes. Coming up with your *ten year intention* could take hours, days, weeks, even months of working and reworking your ideal future scene before you're satisfied.

Once that's done, then comes the fun part. When you know everything you possibly can about that future goal, the next step is to work backward. If you have a ten-year goal, start another paper listing all the facets you will need in eight years to reach that ten-year goal. What will you need to have learned, obtained, done? Then do the same for six years, then four years, then two. What will you have to accomplish in the next year to eventually reach that two-year goal? Then take a look at the next six months, then this next month, and this next week. Then, finally, make a to-do list for tomorrow.

A lot of work? Absolutely! This is not an easy process. The road to mastery never is. But the key here is, *it is doable*!

Ronnie Clemmer: The one thing I wish everybody understood is that 90 percent is process. For an actor, it is the process of getting an agent, getting a manager, getting the job, getting to the auditions, getting prepared. For producers, it is getting materials, getting them set up at the networks or the studios, getting a writer, getting a script, getting a rewrite, getting a star attached. In other words, about 90 percent of what you do is about the *getting there*, it is not about the *being there*. If you don't like the getting there, then you should get out. If it is too painful for you to go to the auditions, to wait for calls, to be doing the acting classes on the side while you are waiting, if it is too painful for you as a reporter to be writing the stuff, preparing it, doing the reading to prepare yourself before you go to the interview, if it is too painful for you as a director or a producer to look for the material, to develop the material, to make the deals and to work out the business, then you shouldn't be in the business. Only 10 percent of it is about making the film. Even that involves 70 percent pre-production, post-production, making sure that you have the right number of chicken legs and drumsticks and stuff for lunch, making sure that the catering guy remembered to bring that special spearmint gum that the star wants every single day. You better like the details of this life, the process of this process, or else you are in the wrong place. If you are waiting for that great film to justify everything you have done, you will end up bitter, angry, uptight and neurotic for most of your life. It is not worth it.

You might find at the end of this process that the path leading to your goal is unacceptable to you, that, in fact, after looking at everything it entails, you no longer have a desire for that intention. On the other hand, you might realize that it's easier than you thought it would be to obtain your ideal scene, and that you now have a clear path to follow. In any case, the exercise itself will be a rewarding experience.

QUALITY KEYS

- *Winners learn how to live with their "inner critics" successfully*: It is a part of being human and there is no practical way to make it simply disappear.

- *Study history's great achievers.* It is sometimes easier to deal with and overcome one's personal fears and frustrations when placed in context with the human frailties and the obstacles endured by history's great achievers.

- *A few facets that help define the very essence of a winner*:

- *The willingness to continue* on a path toward resolution and success, even when faced with life's obstacles.

- *The choice to ignore* the naysayers and to play against the odds.

- *The decision to act like a winner*, to think like a winner and to feel like a winner.

- *Intention*: The product of attention directed to an object of knowledge.

- *Intention is a key element in success.* Set short-term and long-term goals with target dates for completing those goals. Creating *intentions* to follow is the best recipe for consistent and long-lasting achievements.

- *Intention is a key element in learning.* If your intention in study is to do nothing more than pass tests, your time is being wasted on that endeavor. If, however, your intention is to learn the material for practical application in your career or in day-to-day living, it is likely you will retain much more of that information and have a greater comprehension and appreciation for the subject.

- *Intention spin-off.* The by-product of striving for a goal. Without the effort to realize intentions, breakthroughs do not occur. Having intentions and striving to attain goals can never be a losing proposition if one realizes the benefits inherent in the journey toward obtaining those goals.

• *Decide who and what you would like to be in ten or twenty years.* Write down your intentions, both long-term and short-term goals. Your ability to hit a target is directly proportional to the clarity with which you see that target.

• *90 percent is process.* If you are waiting for that great film to justify everything you have done, you will end up bitter, angry, uptight and neurotic for most of your life. It's not worth it.

3 Talk to Me Like the Rain and Let Me Listen

"There are painters who transform the sun into a yellow spot, but there are others who, thanks to their art and intelligence, transform a yellow spot into the sun."

—Pablo Picasso

History's positive and uplifting cultural milestones are stamped with the speeches of fascinating communicators. Abraham Lincoln advanced the abolition of slavery in the United States with his Gettysburg address. Christopher Columbus persuaded King Ferdinand and Queen Isabella to finance his famous voyage. Patrick Henry's fiery speeches, including the famous "I know not what course others may take, but as for me, give me liberty or give me death," made him one of the central figures of the American Revolution. And primarily through oratory, Muhammad, Jesus Christ, and Buddha established and promulgated the world's three biggest religions.

Unfortunately, powerful communication is not the sole possession of the "good guys." Through the ages, the human race has had its share of malevolent communicators who proved to be just as manipulative and just as mighty. Consider the ranting of Genghis Khan, Julius Caesar, and Caligula. How was it possible for Mussolini to convince the Italians that fascism was all the rage, or for Hitler to move a nation to murder six million Jews and instigate a world war? Was it really their messages that engendered obedience? Was it the raw data they had to impart, or are there other components in the makeup of a communicator that urge people to listen, elements far beyond the literal word, that inspire and incite?

I submit that what makes communicators compelling is not the data they have to impart. It is rather the quintessential parts of themselves, interwoven throughout that data that make them fascinating. It is the ability to present material saturated with aspects of their unique personalities. Understanding and utilizing this seemingly simple concept is the cornerstone of a communicator's power.

TENNESSEE CORE

Let's flash back to 1979 for a moment. The University of Tennessee hosted a visit by Tennessee Williams, and asked that I direct a Williams piece as part of the program. Aware that Tennessee had seen most of his works performed innumerable times, I assumed there would be nothing I could create that he hadn't already experienced. Fancying myself an artistic rebel at the time, I still wanted to impress the city of Knoxville, even if getting a rise out of Mr. Williams was a lost cause.

I decided to direct *Talk to Me Like the Rain and Let Me Listen* because of its visceral nature. I cast a wonderfully volatile actor, Mike Miller, to play the male lead. As karma would have it, Mike told me just before the first performance that he had contracted a stomach virus and had been throwing up all morning. (Just what a director wants to hear a half-hour before show time.) I suggested we cancel the show, but Mike wouldn't hear of it. He felt the sickness was under control and didn't want to deprive the cast of the opportunity to perform for the legendary Tennessee Williams.

During the show, I sat on the edge of my seat like a nervous spectator at Wimbledon, bobbing my head back and forth between two potential disasters. I had an actor onstage who might at any moment collapse in a fevered heap. In the audience, I had an author who looked like he just might fall asleep. Tennessee sat placidly during much of the performance, with what seemed a Mona Lisa expression plastered on his face. As I contemplated sneaking out early to commit suicide, the ugliest nightmare a director could possibly imagine came to life right before my eyes. You know the nightmare I'm talking about. The one where the lead actor in the project you've been sweating blood to direct suddenly vomits into a garbage pail onstage during the middle of the performance, while the author, who just happens to be one of the greatest playwrights our planet has ever known, is watching? Yeah, *that* director's nightmare.

Actually, Mike handled his momentary pathology quite well. He incorporated it beautifully into the scene and seamlessly moved on to finish the play. The audience gasped appropriately, thinking it was part of the piece. And Tennessee,...well, Tennessee laughed. Not a titter, not a chuckle—the man guffawed. Out loud and uncontrollably. Not exactly the reaction I had hoped for, and certainly not provoked by any creative directorial vision on my part. But Tennessee Williams was actually moved. And I, in turn, was amazed.

Later, when I had a moment alone with Mr. Williams, I related my surprise and wonder at his reaction. His response sparked for me another of those strange and wondrous life-altering perceptions.

Tennessee grinned like the Cheshire cat. He said, "It wasn't the play, son. Not my words. That boy's pain came from the core. And it just spoke to me."

And it hit me. The one moment that touched this man was the one truly spontaneous moment in the play. It was real, it was pure, and it came deep from the actor's "core." That pure element, mixed in with the material, "spoke" to the audience. I realized then that it was not enough to want to affect others. Somehow, the communicator must find a way to connect and intertwine personal core qualities with the material. If the communicator is affected, it is more likely that the audience will also be affected.

IT'S A GIVEN

Before we go on, let's try a little experiment. The next exercise requires that you first take a moment to think about a personality from your past who deeply inspired you or made a lasting impression on you. The person you conjure up should be someone other than a parent. Instead, pick a teacher, a performer, an inspirational speaker, a priest, whomever. It doesn't matter whether the influence you derived from this individual was positive or negative, and it doesn't matter if the impact came from a single moment or a lifetime of experiences.

EXERCISE #4

(You'll need paper and pencil for this.)

1. Close your eyes and revisit a past moment with a person who made a vivid impression on your life. Remember why he or she made such an impression. Relive in your mind an event you experienced with that individual, which touched you in some fashion.

2. Quickly write down the person's name and the first word that comes to mind describing that person. Don't over-analyze. It shouldn't be an essay. Don't worry about capturing the person's total essence. Just write a word that represents your first visceral impression of that individual. When you're finished, read on. We'll refer back to this exercise presently.

EXERCISE #5:

(You'll need paper and pencil for this.)

Next, take a look at the list of personalities below. Most of them should be familiar to you. Take out a blank sheet of paper and, after reading each name, quickly jot down the first adjective that comes to mind describing each of these individuals. They should not be job descriptions (i.e., doctor, cop, plumber, etc.) but honest adjectives. Don't edit yourself. Don't be concerned about the "best" answer. There is no right or wrong here. For each personality it should be your strongest first impression.

Madonna	Hillary Clinton
Tom Cruise	Rosie O'Donnell
Katie Couric	Johnnie Cochran
Louis Farrakhan	Michael Jackson
Spike Lee	Pamela Anderson
Bill Clinton	Will Smith
Barbara Walters	Saddam Hussein
Oprah Winfrey	David Letterman
Nicolas Cage	Rush Limbaugh
Jesse Jackson	Peter Jennings
Robin Williams	Dennis Rodman

Exercise #5 contains quite a dynamic group of individuals: singers, news anchors, actors, lawyers, politicians, religious leaders, talk show hosts, directors, and comedians; a group widely diverse in backgrounds and skills. I would venture to guess your reactions were different for each person. In fact, you might find it fascinating to have a couple of friends complete the same exercise and compare your answers with theirs. (The odds are their responses will be very different from yours and surprisingly telling about your comrades.) In any case, there is a common denominator among these distinct personalities. Whether you love them or hate them, agree or disagree with their particular styles or ideologies, they are all Masters: accomplished, intriguing, controversial, top-of-the-mark and famous.

So why the two exercises? Go back to *Exercise #4* and take a look at the adjective you wrote describing that influential person in your past. Then, scan your notations from the personalities list in *Exercise #5*. If you had friends do the exercise, read their answers again. Chances are you won't see the word *talented* anywhere. Nor are you likely to find the words *skilled* or *expert*. What you will find are words like *intense, funny, charming, sexy, strong, insane, serious, fanatical*, and so on—all phrases describing *qualities* of their personalities.

The fact of the matter is, *talent* is a given. We expect professionals to be skilled in their individual fields. To be a professional, one must associate with and define a specific craft. For the most part, we take their expertise for granted. You might not relish a certain professional's unique approach or ideology, but that individual is playing with "the big boys and girls," and to do so must have attained a certain portion of his or her status through abilities.

You could argue that certain individuals don't deserve to have such status; that there are those who have no talent and no skills and "couldn't make their way out of a paper bag," or that they were lucky, or had an influential relative, or blackmailed someone somewhere to get where they are. And you might be right, initially. But longevity is anything but luck. As a Las Vegas high-roller buddy of mine once told me:

> *High Roller:* The question isn't whether your number will hit. The question is will you know what to do with it when it does? Are you really prepared for the opportunity when it arrives? Are you really prepared to win?

Think about that one for a moment . . .*Are You Prepared To Win?*

Questions of skill and work ethic are major considerations for the broadcast news station when hiring an anchor or reporter. The general sentiment on this matter is best summed up by Lucy Himstedt, general manager of WFIE-TV, the NBC affiliate in Evansville, Indiana.[6] Ms. Himstedt explains what she looks for when hiring on-air personnel:

> *Lucy Himstedt:* It's true that when I'm searching for an anchor or reporter, I look for someone with natural on-air ability, even if it's going to require some work to develop. But what I see on the audition tape or the air-check is only one part of the process.
>
> When anchors and reporters come in for an interview I look for something else. I already know how I feel about their on-air presence. I want to know how I feel about them as people. If they are great on-camera, but have bad work ethics, I won't hire them.

As with most news directors and general managers, Ms. Himstedt feels strongly about the right kind of preparation for a career in broadcast journalism, and how a strong work ethic must manifest itself early on:

Lucy Himstedt: The most important thing people just starting out need to find is a way to be prepared for what the real working world in broadcast journalism is going to be like. They should find a mentor, do an internship, do whatever it takes to get in and see, "Is this a career?" They must make that commitment. That it is a career. They should know what the hours are going to be. What the pay is going to be. They should learn how to do everything in the newsroom; secretary, rip scripts, shoot if they have to. Those are the kinds of people who are going to have value. Managers are really looking for that kind of work ethic as much as on-air ability. Because so much of the work is not on the air. Work that requires good news judgment and good common sense.

So, number one would be to find out, "Is this something I really want to do?" If anyone gets into this profession just to be on television, go find something else. Do commercials. There is too much work a person might not even be aware of that goes into success.

The desire to hire top professionals, predicated on the assumption that they should already be extremely skilled in their craft and facile at using their talents, is also very evident in the entertainment industry. Vahan Moosekian, who has for many years been an executive producer for studios like Tri-Star and Columbia Pictures,[7] is very frank about his considerations when deciding which actors to hire or work with during his projects:

Vahan Moosekian: I've had the pleasure of working with Albert Finney and George C. Scott and a few other really great actors. You come to realize why they are stars: because they do their job, they do it well, and they do it professionally.

Most English actors tend to be extremely professional in their work ethic. Some people think that Lawrence Olivier was the greatest actor in the world, and some people think that Marlon Brando is the greatest actor in the world. But these two actors approach their craft from two totally different directions. Brando works the craft from the inside out and Olivier worked the craft from the outside in. Ideally, you eventually get to the same place; a performance that is totally believable and captivating and interesting, that you just can't take your eyes off of. I don't think that one school is any better than the other.

The worst kind of actor thinks he is really great, thinks he is so fabulous, acts so arrogant, and is unprofessional in his work ethic and dependability. And is not that good to begin with! You will only put up with classic Brando or classic Robert DeNiro if you get great Brando and DeNiro! When you get an actor who may act like them but can't deliver the goods, you tend to resent that actor.

So television and film producers will go out of their way to find actors who are not only creative but also very professional in how they carry themselves, on and off the set. And the general consensus is that this discipline in craft and self is learned very early on in the actor's development.

Vahan Moosekian: My advice to actors is, don't imitate the behavior of stars unless you are one. And the real bottom line is, know your craft! I have found that actors who are the easiest to work with are the least problematic. Eli Wallach, George C. Scott, Albert Finney, Glenda Jackson, and Dirk Bogarde, all these people I worked with were never problematic. It came from being secure in themselves and what they were going to do.

Glenda Jackson knows her craft, knows her part, and is secure in herself as an artist, so there is no flaky behavior, no running off and not telling anybody where she is going, no, "I have to have my entourage!" She comes and she does her job. She is secure and she likes doing it. I can say that of all the really great actors I have worked with. The ones most secure in their craft are never any trouble.So my advice to actors is always be a damn good craftsman! Know the work well. Know that you know it. It is not enough to know the work. Know that you know it so that you don't drive everybody nuts with your insecurity. The insecurity of stars who have to be treated like stars is because they don't know that they are good and don't feel that they are good. So they need all the trappings of stardom to make them feel important. The best actors to work with are the ones who know their craft well.

The point, then, is not how you got into a coveted position. Whether you knocked on a thousand doors until someone agreed to give you a chance or you were discovered while strolling through the zoo ultimately doesn't matter. What matters is your preparation for that moment. Have you done everything needed to be done to prepare yourself? Have you studied and honed your talents and skills to the best of your abilities? If the ball is handed to you, are you truly ready to run with it? The old adage, "Be careful what you wish for..." suggests that people are usually not prepared to handle dreams that become reality. If you play the game, be prepared to win!

QUALITY

So, if talent is a given, what is the key? If it is assumed that everyone on the playing field knows how to play the game and plays it well, what makes one player stand out from the rest?

The answer is *Quality*: Quality of character, qualities of personality; the qualities that come from the core of the individual; the qualities that individual has attached to the work. You answered it yourself with the above exercises. There is a basic concept one must embrace at the beginning of the journey toward the mastery of communication:

> *Communicators are remembered for*
> *their* **quality***, not their talent.*

This isn't to suggest that communicators should not be skilled or that they should not continually hone their talents. Great singers and dancers take classes when they're not performing. Great lawyers and architects periodically take seminars to keep their abilities sharp. Knowing and being proficient in all the techniques of the game is a basic requirement of the professional, but that's not what sets him apart from **The Pack**. Coach George Karl, currently the head coach of the Milwaukee Bucks, and named "the winningest coach in NBA history" after reaching his 500th win in 1998, shared this with me regarding his philosophy about winners:

Coach George Karl: I am still amazed that in any level of basketball, the player that knows how to play harder than the opponent usually is successful. And the competitive intensity of the game is still one of the top two criteria of success. The other criterion is your team. That's the wonderful nature of basketball: it's a team sport and it's a game of competition. And the competition must be directed at playing hard and playing hard at the maximum intensity for as much of the game as you possibly can.

There is an edge that comes from the combination of being a talented athlete and a great competitor. And then there's the edge of different players at different positions. And as a coach you have to fit those personalities together and go in the direction you want to go on any given night. But the edge comes from a confidence that is gained through playing hard and playing as a team. There's very little confidence in selfish basketball. There's very little confidence in the game when you know you're being outworked by an opponent. Confidence comes when there's a subtle belief that you're doing the right thing and you're playing the right way and you're delivering the right stuff. On TV everybody thinks it's talent that wins. And the truth most of the time is, it's the team that believes, the team that's together that wins.

Yes, we absolutely want our athletes, lawyers, entertainers, politicians, doctors, etc., to be highly trained and skilled. But given a choice between the accomplished doctor who is technically proficient and the accomplished doctor who really seems to love the job and has a great bedside manner, we will opt for the latter. What sets the professional apart from all the rest is not merely his talent. It is his *quality*. It is how he performs and uses his talent, not the talent alone.

BORN TO BE WILD

The 1960s and early '70s will be remembered as one of the best and worst eras in United States history, marked by political intrigues, presidential *faux pas*, the Bay of Pigs invasion, the space-race, the Cuban missile crisis, the generation gap, the Vietnam war, the Watergate affair, increased drug use and abuse, the "hippie" movement, the sexual revolution, the Kennedy and King assassinations, cover-ups, race riots, and heavy-metal music that "the establishment" decided would be the ultimate destruction of our youth.

Some would argue that this highly charged arch in our country's chronicles signified the beginning of the end for our society. Others will tell you that it was just a growing-pain, necessary for tearing down old systems and ideologies to make way for a brighter future. Considering myself a product of that age, I would like to think it was the latter. "Steppenwolf," a popular rock group in the mid-sixties, wrote a song that embodied the sentiments of a "new" generation:

> *Take the world in a love embrace.*
> *Fire all of the guns at once and*
> *Explode into space.*
> *Born To Be Wild!*

The drive to make the world a better place through that "wild" energy of youth, and the fervency of conviction, permeated this country as well as much of Europe. In turn, these passions produced some of the most compelling communicators the world has every known. If you are truly interested in becoming a better communicator, do yourself a favor and review old footage from that era. Try not to get caught up in the rhetoric or become judgmental regarding the era's political and social views. Stay focused on the effects of the speakers' passion on their speech, and, in turn, how it affected their listeners. I have already quoted Martin Luther King, Junior's speech from the 1963 civil rights march on Washington, D.C. It is not hard to see in that speech that King's deepest convictions were wrapped around his words, making them unforgettable.

Another fascinating communicator of the time was John F. Kennedy. Like King, Kennedy would impassion audiences with emotional tones and coining one unforgettable phrase after another. One of his most memorable phrases is, of course, "Ask not what your country can do for you; ask rather what you can do for your country!"[8] In another favorite speech of mine, Kennedy gave a "call to arms" to the Massachusetts State legislature:

John F. Kennedy: Of those to whom much is given, much is required. And when at some future date the high court of history sits in judgment on each of us, recording whether in our brief span of service we fulfilled our responsibilities to the state, our success or failure in whatever office we hold will be measured by the answers to four questions: First, were we truly men of courage? Second, were we truly men of judgment? Third, were we truly men of integrity? Finally, were we truly men of dedication?

Fascinating communication in the 1960s was not limited to mainstream politics and religion. Sounding off their passions as the touchstone for their convictions became the signature of such "troublemakers" as Abbie Hoffman, Timothy Leary, Jane Fonda, Alan Ginsburg, and Lenny Bruce.

Muhammad Ali, former heavyweight champion of the world, changed the face of boxing with his colorful and daring communications. His use of the media to aggressively taunt and challenge his opponents, with claims like *"I am the greatest!"* and *"Float like a butterfly, sting like a bee!"* infused the sport with more excitement for the marginal sports fan, and enticed a nation into watching the televised bouts. The fervor Ali's communications created made him a recognizable figure throughout the world, and paved the way for other athletes to do the same. Today, thirty years later, you will find in all areas of sports that the athlete who knows, understands, and has mastered the art of communication—especially through the media—can promote and build a career far beyond the boundaries of any athletic arena.

SCHOOL'S OUT

In general, people love to learn. Our drive to experience things new and exciting separates us from most of the other creatures on this planet. Now, what's most interesting here is that the same people who love to learn usually hate to be taught. They don't like the feeling of someone pointing an "I told you so" finger at them while droning on about the value of abstinence, or moderation, or sin, or bran cereal, or whatever. They don't want to be criticized and they don't want someone reminding them of their mortality. They just want to be respected and treated like adults. They want people talking *with* them, not *at* them. They want this respect regardless of their age and life experience. This is a big reason why many teenagers regard parents and schoolteachers as living nightmares. It is also the reason why many of these so-called mentors are not the effective communicators one would assume from their titles. Possessing knowledge or position is no guarantee that the people who should be listening will want to listen. And if they do want the information, the guardian, tutor, or coach who must communicate it had better find a way to deliver it that doesn't involve cramming it down the listener's throats.

Coach George Karl: There are times you must be the dictator. But if you try to be the dictator all the time you will probably get rebellion. So a big key is the ability to motivate the team's attitude on a daily basis. And the old philosophy of a positive mental attitude and an energized attitude every day is important in a long, eighty-two-game season. Energy, a positive attitude and communication allow people to grow. Those elements create an environment for improvement.

In the locker room, right before a game, I'll speak to them for about ten minutes. Usually I emphasize the priorities of the game plan with a little bit of motivation, ending with some substantial characteristic of basketball that I think is important from the standpoint of pride. Sometimes it's about attitude or overcoming or persevering or defeating the negative. I don't flood them with a long motivational speech. I try to combine 50 percent motivation with 50 percent game plan, then bring it all together with a positive speech of "kick somebody's butt" or "remember this story" or "think about that."

Many coaches use losing as a time to whip their team, or vent their anger and their frustration and their emotion, but the great coaches use losing as a teacher. It's one avenue coaches can use to deliver confidence to players.

At one point during my sophomore season at Carolina, I remember being in a shooting slump. One day after practice, I was shooting and Coach Smith rebounded the ball for me for about twenty-five minutes. He never said a word. He just threw the ball back at me. When it was over, just before he turned and walked away, he said five words I'll never forget: "I know you can shoot." And that's all he said. And it echoed. And it was such a confidence booster. I don't think he ever had to pick up my confidence ever again.

So one secret of coaching is how you deliver confidence to your players. How you make sure they know you believe in them.

It is a vicious cycle. Many of the mentors we had growing up were bad examples of good communication. Because they were not trained communicators, they would often rely on the accuracy of their data to be the driving force of their communication. Those "teachers" were in the center of **The Pack**. "Why waste time and energy figuring out ways to intrigue, entertain, or motivate? Just give 'em the facts!" The justification for lackluster presentations was that "the truth" should be enough to hold interest. And so the youth of our country, albeit bored out of their collective skulls, assumed that a monotonous presentation was an acceptable form of communication. And that those rare individuals who were Master Communicators, though exciting and fun to experience, were an aberration of nature—probably from some distant galaxy—great to watch and listen to but impossible to emulate because they just weren't human.

So now as adults, when it comes time to perform our communications, the tendency is to fall into the same pattern of **The Pack** we grew up listening to. It's easy, it's safe, and it's acceptable. And what the heck—we endured it all those years and survived. What's good for the goose is good for the gander!

THE ROAD LESS TRAVELED

Of course there are those who decide that the road to mastery is not a forbidden path. They realize that it can be traveled as long as one is dedicated and fervent about the message. And they are the communicators who usually excel in their chosen fields. Take, for example, the following:

- *Walter Cronkite*, who seared the world's tragic and triumphant events into the hearts and minds of our nation with such emotional accounts as John F. Kennedy's final moments in Dallas, and Neil Armstrong's first steps on the moon.

- *Fidel Castro, Benito Mussolini, Adolf Hitler,* and other successful revolutionaries and rulers came to power by understanding the needs and wants of the lower and middle classes. They attracted and galvanized supporters through fiery, dramatic communication, suggesting that they embodied the same basic human desires and promising to deliver those necessities through a unique brand of leadership.

- *Bill Clinton, Ronald Reagan,* United States Senators, United States Congressmen, et al: See Fidel Castro, Benito Mussolini, Adolf Hitler, above.

- *Marlon Brando* popularized the naturalistic "method" style of acting in this country by finding the down-to-earth, human qualities in his portrayals of every character.

- *Susan B. Anthony* devoted fifty years of her life to speaking out for women's suffrage. Her orations gave birth to the National Woman's Suffrage Association, the newspaper named *Revolution,* and the women's rights movement in this country.

- *Clarence Darrow* was an American lawyer best known for his defense of John Scopes, who was charged with teaching the theory of evolution in a Tennessee high school. Darrow was opposed to capital punishment, and his passionate communications assured that none of his clients, including fifty accused murderers, ever received the death penalty.

- *Billy Graham* is an American evangelist and leading spokesman for Fundamentalism. Graham's charismatic communications are known the world over, his followers numbering in the millions.

- *Henry Kissinger* was the first foreign-born citizen to hold the post of secretary of state. Kissinger's communications helped put an end to the Vietnam War; subsequently, he won the Nobel Prize for peace in 1973.

The list goes on and on. Choose your fascinating communicators. No matter their message, no matter their vocation, no matter their gender,

race, or religion, a common characteristic binds them: It is the passionate belief in themselves and their message. That passion allows Master
Communicators to connect their core, and therefore their quality, to the
material. That *Core Quality* is what is human about the communication.
In turn, those human sensibilities are what the listener relates to and
ultimately agrees with.

Personal Intentions

To help crystallize your *intentions* on the journey toward mastery, take a few moments to make a communicators/descriptions list of your own. Make a list of individuals whom you consider fascinating communicators. Not just present-time communicators, but all *The Masters* who come to mind, in all areas of communication throughout history. Beside each of those names, list all the characteristics that make/made them effective. For example:

COMMUNICATOR	DESCRIPTION
Madonna	*Good singing voice, constantly redefines self-style and singing style, creative, song writer, overt sexuality, gutsy, mother, bleached blond, egocentric, stands her ground, etc.*
Mother Teresa	*Short, Albanian, worked in India, founded order of Catholic nuns, selfless, loved the poor, helped the dying, kind, loved fellow man, altruist, etc.*
Howard Stern	*Good broadcast voice, acerbic humor, overt sexuality, gutsy, shock-jock, overbearing, long unkempt hair, etc.*
Barbara Walters	*Good listener, intelligent, speech impediment, stands her ground, self-assured, serious nature, etc.*
David Letterman	*Goofy, standup comedian, gap-toothed, tall, cigar smoker, creative, adorable, messy hair, glasses, talk-show host, former weather man, drives fast, single, etc.*
Shirley MacLaine	*Spiritual, gutsy singer, dancer, book author, redhead, sassy, dynamic, good actor, past lives, etc.*
Meryl Streep	*Mother, activist, actor: brilliant, transparent, erases herself, full of nuance, dialect expert, mannered at times, always kisses men the same way, plays broad range of characters in a natural and compelling way.*

Next, start your own "Personal Intentions: List of Facets" by creating another document with the headings *Intentions* and *Counter-Intentions*. Take all the characteristics you discovered with your communicators/ descriptions list, sans duplicates, and list them under the appropriate headings. If you feel that a certain characteristic is important for you to own or develop, list it under *Intentions*. If it's a characteristic you don't feel will make you the kind of Master Communicator you want to be, list it under *Counter-Intentions*. For example:

PERSONAL INTENTIONS	COUNTER-INTENTIONS
Good voice	*Speech impediment*
Intelligent	*Overt sexuality*
Stands ground	*Egocentric*
Good listener	*Overbearing*
Self-assured	*Past lives*
Spiritua	*Mother*
Good actor	*Singer*
Devilish sense of humor	*Acerbic humor*
Giving	*Bleached blond*
Great smile	*Unkempt hair*
Standup comedian	*Cigar smoker*
And so on.	*And so on.*

Once this is accomplished, the idea is to give each characteristic under the *Personal Intentions* heading a definition that relates to your personal needs and goals, then decide the actions you must take to accomplish those intentions. For example:

Personal Intention	Personal Definition	Personal Actions
Good voice	*Lower, well modulated, great breath support, wide range, etc.*	*Weekly voice class, practice two times each week, etc.*
Self-assured	*Good self-image, confident in front of others, nicely groomed appearance, etc.*	*Exercise every day, better diet, update wardrobe, conversation with one new person every day, public speaking course, etc.*
Intelligent	*Well-read, good vocabulary, versed in many subjects, conversations sound substantive, etc.*	*Obtain library card, read one new book on a different subject every two weeks, read one liberal and one conservative publication (i.e. Newsweek and Time) each week, watch local and national news shows every day, etc.*

In this way you'll begin to have an idea of where you're headed as a Master Communicator. Remember, the clearer the targets, the easier they are to hit. When a target is clearly in your sights, you must then decide if you really want to hit it. How important is it? Is it really worth your time and effort? Once decided, since you've spelled out the actions needed, all that's left is to take those steps.

Now it could be argued that these lists contain superfluous information, such as "past lives" or "mother"—data that seem irrelevant to communication. I would assert however that what people project about themselves in look and station begins to communicate long before one word is ever spoken. Dressed in a business suit, you are more likely to be believed when discussing the stock market than outfitted in a sexy swimsuit. On the other hand, swimsuit-clad and "buffed" might be a preferable look when talking about extreme water sports.

This is not to say that once a list is created, it can never be amended or altered. In fact, as you gain experience, learn, and grow in your particular field and in your life, many of your intentions will surely change. This exercise is just a great springboard to get you started.

Go ahead; give it a shot. Begin your own "Personal Intentions List." Working up your list might take a little time, so don't begin by thinking you have to rush through it or even finish it now. Enjoy the process. Once accomplished, get out your appointment book or wall calendar and schedule your next Personal Intentions List update in six months. As you grow and develop personally and professionally, periodically reworking your Personal Intentions List will be a great way to keep you motivated and on track.

QUALITY KEYS

- *History's milestones* are stamped with the speeches of fascinating communicators.

- *What makes communicators compelling* is not the data they have to impart, but their unique personality wrapped around that data.

- *If the communicator is affected, it is more likely the listener will also be affected.* The communicator must find a way to connect and intertwine personal *core qualities* with the material.

- *Prepare yourself to win.* Study and hone your talents and skills to the best of your abilities. If the ball is handed to you, be ready to run with it!

- *Communicators are remembered for their quality, not their talent*: Quality of character, qualities of personality, qualities from the person's core.

- *Passionate involvement in the message* has produced some of the most compelling communicators the world has ever known.

- *Most people love to learn, but hate the feeling of being taught.*

- *To excel at communication is an attainable goal.* One must only be dedicated and fervent to travel the road toward mastery.

- *There is a common characteristic that binds Master Communicators.* A passionate belief in themselves and their message allows Master Communicators to connect their core and quality to the material. That *core quality* is what is human and dynamic about the communication.

- To help crystallize your *intentions* on the journey toward mastery, create a *"Personal Intentions: List of Facets."*

4 QUALITY CORE

"THERE IS A VITALITY, A LIFE FORCE, A QUICKENING THAT IS TRANSLATED THROUGH YOU INTO ACTION, AND BECAUSE THERE IS ONLY ONE OF YOU IN ALL TIME, THE EXPRESSION IS UNIQUE. AND IF YOU BLOCK IT, IT WILL NEVER EXIST THROUGH ANY OTHER MEDIUM AND BE LOST."
—MARTHA GRAHAM

TELEVISION WRITER/PRODUCERS ARE NOTORIOUS for having strong opinions on just about everything because they're the ones always caught in the middle. On the one hand they have to deal with "the talent," who can be demanding and are almost never pleased. On the other they have to deal with network and/or studio executives, who can be demanding and are almost never pleased. And so it is with Tom Amundsen, a talented and successful writer/producer whose career has also included acting and directing. For the past several years, Tom wrote and produced the ABC television shows *Perfect Strangers* and *Full House*, and recently served as a creative consultant on Paramount Studios' situation comedy, *Sister, Sister*.

I recently spoke with Tom about the thrills and agonies of being a writer/producer in Hollywood. His perspectives on industry politics and working with networks, studio executives, and actors are fascinating. Above all, they highlight the necessity for understanding discipline, core, training, and attitude for those interested in becoming Master Communicators.

Tom Amundsen: Everything in this business is personality. Everybody has their own distinct personality. Everybody has their own thing that they bring, whether it is that someone is good with story or is good with jokes. Everybody brings different sensibilities, different morals, and different ideas.

The thing you have to realize is that when you are writing for a sitcom, you have to turn your humor and sensibilities and your core into the core of the character you are writing for. What you are doing is writing for the core of a nonexistent person. It is somebody who has been created. The actors who play the parts will also bring their essence and things into the characters, their take on it. So, you are writing for the actors and the characters. I worked on *Full House* for three years, and coming up with jokes for the Olsen twins is a lot different than coming up with jokes for *Frasier*. You can adapt yourself to doing either one because I believe that funny is funny and a joke is a joke. I believe there is a way in telling it. I believe that if something is funny and I tell it, it can also be funny if someone else tells it. But not everybody can tell it funny. Like anything else, you mold it to your sense of humor.

In acting, anybody can read a line of Shakespeare. But not everybody can make sense out of a line of Shakespeare. It is the same thing with a joke. God knows I'm not equating *Full House* with *The Taming of the Shrew*, but it is the same thing. Not everything is funny. There are a lot of times that you will come up with a funny joke and the actor can't do it. It is all personality-based, especially in TV, because there are not a lot of good actors in TV.

Here's an interesting thing about "personalities" versus "core." Studios are throwing deals at standup comics right now because of Roseanne, because of Tim Allen, because of Jerry Seinfeld, to a certain extent Ellen DeGeneres, and Brett Butler. These people have had huge success with their TV shows. So the executives and network people who are basically "suits,"—bottom-line people who think they are creative but all they see is a standup comic who is successful—will say, "Get me another standup comic!" They don't realize that all those people that I mentioned, Roseanne, Tim Allen, and Seinfeld, are not just "personalities." They spent years on the road honing that character and finding that "core" of who that character is. They all came with a very specific voice, a very specific idea of who they were. That is why their shows are successful, because they know who those characters are! And those characters have a very specific, well-defined *Quality Core*.

Nowadays they just get standup comics and throw them in a show. And they are not actors. Actors you can give funny lines to and they can make them funny. People who are not trained as actors or communicators, you can't just give them funny lines if they don't know how to deliver them. If you are basing lines on who they are and characters they have created, and you are writing to their "core" and their personalities, it's a lot easier to make a Tim Allen funny, or a Roseanne funny, or a Brett Butler funny. If a studio takes a standup comic off the road and shoves him into what my vision of what a sitcom should be, the standup has no idea of how to do that.

The most successful actors bring themselves to their work, from the moment of audition through the moment of performance. The most successful actors are the natural actors.

I sit through auditions all the time. I like it when an actor comes in and says, "Hi, how are you, it's good to see you," and then just does the scene for me—just shows me what he wants to do with the scene. Most actors don't do that. They come in and go on about how we have a friend in common, we've got this and that and it's totally unnatural. They don't get it that actors are their own worst enemies. I know they are because I used to be one! There were times when I used to do that. You think you have an "in" because you know a friend of the guy who walked the casting director's dog once. Just show me your work!

That kind of stuff comes through in the performance, too. Don't be a phony. If you try something and it doesn't work, don't apologize because it was totally wrong. Just try something else. Don't take yourself so seriously. Be yourself. That is the only thing you can bring to a character. I don't care how much training you've had. I don't care how many other jobs you have had. If I have a character for you, the only thing you can bring to that character is yourself. If you can't be yourself then you aren't going to be able to do it.

Well, what is it? We've mentioned it a few times. We've talked around it quite a bit. Mr. Amundsen suggests it to be essential for the actor, and I've suggested it to be the life's blood of the master. So, what exactly is *Quality Core?*

To appreciate the dynamics of Quality Core (or anything, for that matter) it is beneficial to start with the rudiments. Break the thing down to its essentials, fully understand the building blocks, and then put it back together again. Before we determine the power of Quality Core, let's take a look at the specific attributes that formulate your core and its qualities.

The dictionary tells us that *core* can be defined as:

1. **The innermost part of anything.**
2. **The most important part.**
3. **Heart; center; essence.**

Of the many definitions for *quality*, the ones I find most appropriate for the purposes of this discussion are:

1. **A characteristic or distinguishing attribute.**
2. **The natural or essential character of something.**
3. **Excellence; superiority.**

By intertwining these two concepts, we can begin to define the cornerstone of one's personality. Like snowflakes, every human being is said to be singly different from every other. Even though two people may have the same outer appearance, each will have a different center, composed of characteristics that are uniquely mixed and formulated. Therefore, the essential qualities inherent in an individual's core are what make up that person's being.

CORE QUALITIES:

*1. The attributes, features, or traits inherent in the
natural or essential character of a person.*
*2. The distinct and personal formulation of those characteristics,
channeled through the physical being, is what distinguishes
or identifies each individual as unique.*

What are the "attributes, features, or traits" of core qualities? Do all of us have different qualities, or do we all possess the exact same qualities and just express them in different ways? To make an analogy, it could be argued that one chef's materials are much like any other's. Those would include fruits, vegetables, meats, dairy products, spirits, spices, pots and pans, cooking utensils, a stove, etc. But what turns the ordinary fare of one cook into the extraordinary Epicurean delight of another? What makes the core qualities of one individual the *Quality Core* of another?

A Drop of the Ocean

There are essentially two layers that make up an individual's core. The first layer comprises all human emotions. That's right, *all* human emotions. In fact, there are psychologists who would tell you that by the age of six, most children have already experienced every emotion in the Human Condition, and that those emotions become indelibly seared into the child's being.

"Not possible," you proclaim! You say that to this day you've never won a gold medal at the Olympics, or murdered someone in jealousy. So how could you possibly know what those heightened emotions of victory or rage would feel like? Even now, much less when you were six!

Richard Boleslavsky, the legendary acting teacher of the Moscow Art Theatre and the American Laboratory Theatre, wrote a wonderful book for beginning actors, called *Acting: The First Six Lessons*. In it he explains that an actor does not need the actual experience of strangling someone to play a murderer. Boleslavsky makes the argument that if you've ever killed a bug, you have the capacity to play the roll of Othello. His point is that murder is murder, no matter to what degree; that in essence, a drop of the ocean is still the ocean. And once you've experienced any particular emotion, you should be able to call on it again at any time, manipulate its intensity, and use it as you please in your craft.

I will go Boleslavsky one better. Emotions linger just below the surface. They are constantly running through us. Like high-strung greyhounds waiting for the bell to sound and the gates to fly open, our emotions are poised and waiting for the next experience that will allow them to break free.

I know, it sounds pretty dramatic, but think about it. Think about the last time you were suddenly touched by a piece of music, or found yourself chuckling as you experienced someone's infectious laughter, or angrily blurted out an obscenity as some idiot cut you off in traffic. Where did the emotion come from? It isn't as if you were thinking about it, consciously holding onto the emotion, hoping for the appropriate moment to spring it on yourself.

Like strings on a harp, any emotion that is possible to experience waits at your core, ready to be plucked. Most of us have fallen victim to the power of our emotions at one time or another. Ever blame emotions for actions you would have never committed had you been thinking "clearly?" Just consider the number of defendants who have used "temporary insanity" as a plea!

A good communicator understands that one should not be controlled by one's emotions, but that core emotions can be used as powerful tools in communication. One of the best explanations I've heard regarding this notion actually comes from the composer/songwriter Stacy Widelitz. A brilliant, creative musician, Stacy has composed hundreds of scores for films and television shows, including the song "She's Like the Wind," awarded as "One of the Most Successful Songs of 1988" and "One of the Most Performed Songs of the Year on Radio and Television." A few years ago, while directing the musical comedy *Circle of Will* in Hollywood, I had the distinct honor and pleasure of collaborating with Stacy, who composed and directed the music. His views on the part emotion plays in communication:

Stacy Widelitz: What makes for interesting communication is the ability, in as few words as possible, to cut to an emotional core of what is trying to be expressed. Thomas Jefferson once said, "The greatest of all talents is never using two words where one will do." I believe that to be absolutely true. Try to present things as clearly and distinctly as possible that convey exactly the feelings you want to elicit.

For the singer, emotional connection is extremely important. The singer who truly believes every word of the lyric he sings is the superior singer. Joe Cocker may not have the greatest voice in the

world but you believe the words that this man is singing. Janis
Joplin was like that. She was not the greatest singer technically, but
the emotional commitment when she sang was remarkable.

Basically, great communication comes down to going with your
instincts. If it elicits a response in me, I have to trust that it's going
to elicit that same response in somebody else. This is for music as
well. The technical part of it is what you discard after a while. You
learn how to do your craft and then you get rid of it. What it comes
down to is expression of emotion. Van Gogh said, "I am trying to
break down the iron wall between what I feel and what I express."
Those are the words that every artist should live by.

So, the Master Communicator never wants to be the victim of core
emotions. Instead, traveling the road to mastery includes learning how
to control those emotions and weave them into a more powerful form of
communication. Later on we will talk about identifying specific emotions in your core, and how to apply them to your craft. First, let's
uncover the other layer of *core*.

Every Character In Search of a Person

You speak to a lover in certain tones you would never use with your boss.
You converse differently with a parent than you do with kids. The
person you become to complete a sales transaction is quite different from
the demeanor you project on a first date. So, which is the real you? And
which characters are lies, "masks" that you wear, not really connected
to your core?

The truth is they are all "you" to some degree. Literally hundreds of
personalities make up your core: parent, adult, child, boss, servant,
lover, wallflower, philanthropist, misanthrope, liberal, conservative,
etc. Some of these characters are more accessible than are others, but
they are all *Core Personalities* and can be tools of the Master Communicator. To better understand the roles of these Core Personalities, they are
divided here into three groups:

CORE PERSONALITIES

- *Primary Core Characters*
- *Secondary Core Characters*
- *Tertiary Core Characters*

Primary Core Characters, or PCCs, are personalities you have developed by actually being those characters at certain points in your life. For instance, presumably you went through the stages of childhood and pubescence to become the person you are today. Those two identities have not vanished but are still part of your core. Although we are no longer children, the experiences of youth are now imbedded as the "child" within us. Our high school years may have implanted a "rebellious teen" personality or "football jock" personality as a PCC. The experience of waiting tables to get through college forms a specific character that remains in the core. PCCs are the strongest characters that make up your core and much of your day-to-day routine. PCCs can be consciously chosen for a particular situation but are so close to the surface that, often, they are involuntary reactors to emotionally charged situations.

PCC EXAMPLES

Conscious choice: Having friends over for a fancy dinner, you become the gracious host, gourmet cook and attentive food server at various times during the evening—all characters you have cultivated in your past, consciously brought to the forefront for a particular situation.

Unconscious choice: Caught in a lie, your heart races uncontrollably and your demeanor changes to that of you as a small child, caught "with your hand in the cookie jar." The confrontation is uncomfortable because your "child" finds it hard to make eye contact or speak in normal tones. Afterward, you chide yourself for not having more control of the situation and acting like such a kid!

EXERCISE #6:

(You'll need paper and pencil for this.)

Take a moment to reflect on the characters in your core. Come up with three PCCs that inhabit your core, and jot them down. Next to each character, note an example illustrating how that personality manifests itself in your life.

Secondary Core Characters, or SCCs, are personalities you have experienced firsthand to such a degree that you can easily become them, sometimes without thinking. The most obvious SCC would be a parent. Another might be a best friend. Living with someone or experiencing someone for an extended period of time can put its stamp on your core. The personality eventually seeps into your being and becomes its own separate character.

SCC EXAMPLES:

Conscious choice: Your favorite high school coach motivated you to succeed by a teaching style mixing high expectations and strict demands with humor and anecdotes. Now, when called upon to teach, you incorporate the very same style. Even though you haven't practiced this approach, you are confident and comfortable with employing it when needed.

Unconscious choice: You get angry at your kids and blurt out a reprimand, then cover your mouth in horror as you realize you just sounded exactly like one of your parents.

EXERCISE #7:

(You'll need paper and pencil for this.)

Identify three SCCs that inhabit your core, and jot them down. Next to each character, note an example illustrating how that personality manifests itself in your life.

Tertiary Core Characters, or TCCs, are the plethora of personalities you have marginally experienced over the course of a lifetime. These personalities include friends, relatives, media celebrities, fictional characters, imaginary childhood friends, etc.

TCCs are not dominant, and take a conscious effort to call to the forefront of your core. The utilization of TCCs may take more focus and stronger concentration, but they are still viable tools for the Master Communicator.

TCC EXAMPLES:

Conscious choice: It is not within your PCCs or SCCs to be "outgoing." However, you have witnessed your uncle being the life of the party often enough to know what people find charming. When forced, you dredge up those experiences to get you through awkward social situations.

Conscious choice: You go to a costume party dressed as Dracula. You've seen the movies and read the books. Acting like the guy is a piece of cake. In fact, you have so much fun being this personality that by the end of the night, you've left your mark on every neck in the house. The next day you go out to lunch with your friends, who congratulate you for being so convincing. (And for some strange reason they all order meals drenched in garlic butter.)

EXERCISE #8

(You'll need paper and pencil for this.)

Identify three TCCs that inhabit your core, and jot them down. Next to each character, note an example illustrating how that personality manifests itself in your life.

WHEELS OF FORTUNE

Now that we have a better understanding of the personalities (PCCs, SCCs, and TCCs) that inhabit our core, what those personalities are and how those personalities are established and formed, let's get back to our original definition of *core qualities*. We now know that core qualities...

1. (The attributes, features, or traits inherent in a person's natural or essential character) are actually the myriad human emotions plus the personalities (PCCs, SCCs and TCCs) that make up a person's core. Let me repeat that because it is important:

$$Core\ Qualities = Emotions + (PCCs,\ SCCs,\ and\ TCCs)$$

The core qualities of an individual equal the totality of human emotions plus that person's primary, secondary and tertiary core characters.

The emotions in your core are common to nearly all human beings. What makes individuals unique are their particular PCCs, SCCs and TCCs and how those core characters mix with human emotions. If we look at a graphic representation of how core qualities outwardly manifest themselves at any given moment, we see that the coupling of character to emotion gives us the possibility of innumerable combinations for present-time behavior.

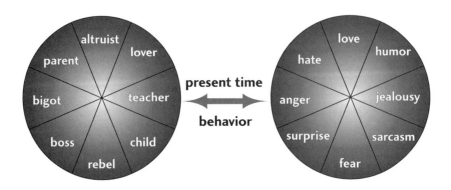

This representation of a person's core character element (Teacher) aligning and hooking up with a core emotional element (Anger) is a simplification of the bigger, more complex paradigm that actually exists. Not only are there thousands of emotions and characters to choose from, there are shades of each and the ability to play variations of those shades, simultaneously. Thus, each of us has the potential for delivering many forms of dynamic communication. The possibilities are endless.

If you consider that mind-boggling, just take a closer look at the second half of our core qualities definition:

2. *The distinct and personal formulation of those characteristics, channeled through the physical being, is what distinguishes or identifies each individual as unique.*

Not only do you have an infinite number of possible personalities, but also your physical features set you apart from anyone else on this planet. (Even "identical" twins are not exactly identical.) Those physical features, coupled with the particular way your muscles move to create facial expressions, hand gestures, and body language, make you a truly one-of-a-kind physical being.

No matter which characters or emotions you choose to express, they will be extraordinary because they must be communicated through your unique physical instrument. So, no matter what you do, no matter how you choose to communicate, it will be special. You are special!

EXERCISE #9:

(You'll need paper and pencil for this.)

Core Qualities = Emotions + (PCCs, SCCs and TCCs)
Here is an example of pairing a core character with an emotion for a particular event:

SCC	Emotion	Event
Parent	Anger	Scolding the dog for tearing up the couch.

Take a look at the characters you identified in exercises 7–9. Define three different Core Qualities by choosing one character from each exercise and pairing it with an emotion. Then note when that match might manifest itself in your daily life.

FLYING

Patrick Swayze's dedication and fervency for the craft of acting are always resolute and often inspiring. While preparing for the role of a skydiver in the film *Point Break*, Patrick naturally learned and perfected the skill of skydiving. Actually, as far as I'm concerned, there is nothing "natural" about jumping out of a plane at 15,000 feet. I personally think it's insane. But if you watch that film, you'll witness an actor who makes aerial acrobatics look as effortless and natural as if he were an eagle.

One night at a dinner party, I jokingly told Patrick that he was insane for voluntarily falling out of planes. His tongue-in-cheek reply held an underlying message that was somewhat sobering and very revealing of his true nature.

Patrick said, "That's the difference between you and me: When you jump out of a plane, you think of falling. When I jump out of a plane, I think of flying."

That's what I mean by inspiring. Patrick's passionate investment in whatever he sets his mind to brings out the best of his core qualities and diminishes those characteristics that might get in the way of his process.

Earlier, I posed the question "What makes the core qualities of one individual the *Quality Core* of another?" With the expert chef, it's the ability to take a look at all the raw materials in any kitchen, identify the ones needed, and use them in the appropriate way and in exactly the right amounts to make the perfect meal. With the communicator, it's the ability to identify and bring to the surface the specific core qualities needed and wanted for a particular situation. And to set aside the core qualities that would get in the way of that communication, so that your core is purely devoted to the success of that particular moment.

Quality Core: 1. The qualities of an individual's core considered premium and best suited for a specific situation or unit of time.

2. The ability to bring to the forefront those superior core qualities specifically attuned to a particular occasion or event.

3. A quality core diminishes undesirable or unnecessary personality characteristics and enhances those traits that allow for the highest performance of an individual.

Most of us have the elements and ability to develop and maintain a *Quality Core*. Few of us actually strive toward that goal because the path is not an easy one. It takes passion, focus, and fervency. It takes a belief in oneself and a love of oneself. It takes the understanding and acceptance that there is no earthly Nirvana, that instead, the road to *Quality Core* is actually a lifelong commitment. And one must enjoy the ride, because, in the end, the experience of that ride is all that matters.

Quality Keys

- *Rudiments*: To fully appreciate and understand a thing, it is beneficial to start with the rudiments. Break the thing down to its essentials, fully understand its building blocks, and then put it back together again.

- *Core*: The innermost part of anything; the most important part; the heart, center or essence of a thing.

- *Quality*: A characteristic or distinguishing attribute; the natural or essential character of something; excellence; superiority.

- *Core Qualities*: The attributes, features, or traits inherent in the natural or essential character of a person. The distinct and personal formulation of those characteristics, channeled through the physical being, is what distinguishes or identifies each individual as unique.

- *Primary Core Characters*: Personalities developed by actually having been those characters during one's life.

- *Secondary Core Characters*: Personalities experienced firsthand to such a degree that a person can easily become them.

- *Tertiary Core Characters*: The plethora of personalities marginally experienced over the course of a lifetime. The utilization of these personalities may take a stronger concentration but are still viable tools for the communicator.

- *Quality Core*: The qualities of an individual's core considered premium and best suited for a specific situation or unit of time.

5 WINDOWS TO THE SOUL

"SECURITY IS MOSTLY A SUPERSTITION. IT DOES NOT EXIST IN NATURE, NOR DO THE CHILDREN OF MEN AS A WHOLE EXPERIENCE IT. AVOIDING DANGER IS NO SAFER IN THE LONG RUN THAN OUTRIGHT EXPOSURE. LIFE IS EITHER A DARING ADVENTURE OR NOTHING."

—HELEN KELLER

NOT LONG AGO MY WIFE AND I SAW A FUN MOVIE about a talking pig, called *Babe*. All of the animals in the film were given human characteristics and spoke English to each other when humans were not present. As we walked out of the theatre, I turned to see that my wife was beaming from the cinematic experience.

She exclaimed, "That was such a sweet film, and Babe was so cute. I don't think I'll ever be able to eat pork again!"

"Strong praise from a Texas girl!" I told her. As we were getting in the car I proposed dinner and asked for any suggestions.

Her afterglow turned into excitement. "Dinner sounds great!" she said. "I'm starved!" Then she thought for a moment and came up with what seemed to her a brainstorm. "You know what I really feel like is a great big juicy hamburger!"

Shocked, I turned to her and asked, "Because the movie was so sweet, you won't eat pig, but you'll eat a cow?"

Mystified that I would ask such a foolish question, she replied, "Now, you know that cow was not a very good actor!"

What compels us toward certain communicators and repels us from others? What makes us want to listen to a select few and devour the rest? What are the elements that make communication understandable, tangible, memorable and effective?

Patrick Swayze: You find it in their eyes. Do they just have a haze as they say their lines, or is it somebody really trying to live and breathe inside of the skin of their character? It takes two to tango. As an actor, you need someone on the other side giving you something. If you don't have that and you can't get that, then it's a whole other game. You've got to find a way not to go into that haze and place someone or something or the right character or person or performance in front of you. So you go blind to what you're seeing, and create a fantasy.

Dick Clark: The visual element is powerful. This "perpetual youth" image has positive and negative aspects. It is intimidating because people are inclined to look at me very closely and say, "How the hell does he look that way?" You don't want to be judged that way. I'm concerned about how close they bring the camera to me now, when I never was before, because I'm inhibited by the fact that I am supposed to look as good as possible. It's a vanity thing. That disrupts my delivery. Usually, what I try to do when I'm with an unfamiliar camera crew is say, "You have to remember that for a guy my age, a close-up starts at the knee." We make a joke about it. I let them know, "If I see you crawling in with an eyeball-to-mouth shot, I'm going to freak!"

Sandra Connell: News directors always ask what my opinion is of somebody they are considering for a position. If I tell them "She's a little stiff," I then ask if they've met her. If they say, "Oh yes, and she's fantastic!" I tell them, "Well, then she'll be okay. If you liked her, if she's smart, and if one-on-one she's fantastic, a talent coach can put that on TV so she'll look more natural."

They really have to talk with their eyes. Their eyes speak volumes. Especially in a news anchor when they're reading TelePrompTer. If they are locked on that prompter you get nothing from their eyes. When they smile, they have to smile with their eyes. Putting it all together is the learned skill. It's great if it's spontaneous, but it doesn't always work that way. You've got to make sure the eyes aren't dead, what we call "prompter stare." The eyes are the windows to the soul.

Even though there are various facets and many different roads that lead to great communication, those communicators we call The Masters understand that certain concepts are universal, transcending style, venue, message, and profession. These truisms can be summed up by three main maxims:

MAXIM #1

*The most powerful element
in communication is* **Visual**

THE EYES HAVE IT

Some years ago, a psychologist named Mehrabian did a study[9] concluding that 55 percent of a speaker's impact during communication is visual, including facial expressions, body language, hair, dress, make-up, surroundings, etc. More than half of communication is based on what we see or what we can get others to see.

It makes perfect sense. It's the way the brain functions. To retain a concept, the brain will first try to visualize that concept. If I were to begin a conversation by saying to you, "The red Corvette has a busted taillight," you wouldn't immediately begin to spell out R-E-D C-O-R-V-E-T-T-E in your head. The first action your brain would take is to create a vision of that car, incorporating the busted taillight. Then it would use that image for reference as you continued to listen to the story. If you had never seen a Corvette before, the brain would do its best to pull from the lifetime collection of images it has of other cars, along with the communicator's verbal description, to create a visual point of reference.

Visual impressions do more to facilitate our understanding and memory retention than do the other senses. If more preschool and elementary school teachers understood and embraced this basic concept, our educational system wouldn't turn out so many mathochists. (*Mathochist* is a word I concocted in high school, meaning "math hater." It isn't a subject I did well in.) Having children memorize tables and equations does little for their comprehension. The intention of such exercises becomes nothing more than regurgitation to pass a test. It is a short-term goal. As discussed in Chapter 2, the intention of learning should be focused on the long-term goal of application. Why not help students solidify their understanding by teaching them addition and subtraction with building blocks? Allow them to discover geometry, supplementing their protractor illustrations by actually constructing three-dimensional geometric figures. These techniques might take longer, but if children demonstrate the process, do it and see it in the physical universe, they are more apt in their daily lives to remember and use the lessons learned.

The massive stockpile of visual images in your brain is constantly being referenced as an initial decision-maker. We will believe what we see before trusting our sense of hearing or even touch. How many times have you seen a woman for the first time and, before she said a word, you already had an opinion about her, just by looking at her? Or a quick glance at a man gave you all the information you felt you needed to know his background, social status, personality, and even his sexual orientation, all before he opened his mouth. And after speaking with him, you still held tightly to your preconceptions even though his voice and speech pattern seemed to communicate a different impression. The visual image is so strong that the brain will want to believe it over anything else it senses.

Master Communicators understand the power of visual elements and use them to initiate the best first impressions, feelings, and style. One such master is Bob Goen, previously a sportscaster, game show host (*Perfect Match* and *Wheel of Fortune*) and master of ceremonies (the Miss Universe Pageant, the Miss USA Pageant, and the Miss Teen USA Pageant). Bob is currently co-host of *Entertainment Tonight*, the #1 syndicated entertainment magazine TV show in America.

Bob Goen: I will do something as simple as scratch my face during a read. That allows me to drop my guard and just be myself. And I think that's what the home audience sees. That's why I think I'm better at television than radio. My sentences are not clear, quickly thought out, every-word-in-its-proper-place kind of sentences. I tend to go circuitously through a sentence. That doesn't translate in radio. But in television, when you have a face to look at and you can see the thought process that takes place in a sentence, it makes more sense. And it's more believable. It's more human. And that's what I always try to get back to.

Fascinating communicators understand the strength of visual elements in their craft. The actor is aware that crying without tears becomes suspect. The news-person realizes the power of a "live shot." And the politician seeks every opportunity to be seen speaking with the "common man" or kissing a baby. Master Communicators are expert in getting you to actually see the concepts they are communicating, whether it be in the physical universe or in your imagination. They know that once you grasp the concept visually, their communication becomes that much more powerful and enduring.

EMOTIONAL TONES

Anthropologists studying ancient cultures have theorized about the origins of human language. Some believe it sprang from various expressions of emotion. Others think it naturally grew out of social behaviors like dancing or working together. In any case, the way we now speak probably had its beginnings with cavemen who attached emotional tones to vocal sounds and combined them with body language. And those barbarians who were especially gifted at flailing about while emoting to the high heavens (even though they had very little to talk about) eventually left the folds of their tribes to band together and form a higher breed of troglodyte known as "politicians." I'm kidding, of course. I don't think they were actually called "politicians" until troglodytes invented the art of joke-telling. (I'm kidding, I'm kidding.)

Politicians have taken a lot of heat over the years for overstating, over-explaining, and being overly dramatic. I would suspect it is because the vast majority of those politicians, the ones who travel in The Pack, envy the few masters who have made their marks in history. And it doesn't matter whether those marks were made with the eloquence of Sir Winston Churchill's emotional speech to the people of Europe when he first introduced the V for Victory hand gesture...

Winston Churchill: The V sign is the symbol of the unconquerable will of the occupied territories, and a portent of the fate awaiting the Nazi tyranny.

...or the pomposity of Soviet leader Nikita Khrushchev's sudden interruption at the United Nations by shouting in Russian, pounding his fist, and then banging a shoe on his delegation's desk during a speech by British Prime Minister Harold Macmillan. The Pack has always realized that history's most successful orators knew how to effectively combine all the elements of communication and deliver them at their peak levels.

For more than twenty years, Rick Dent has specialized in providing strategic communications counsel for politicians. To date, he has directed eighteen political campaigns and served as the press secretary to two governors. Most recently, Mr. Dent led Governor Don Siegelman's upset victory over Alabama Governor Fob James.

Rick Dent: Using visual and emotional tones together can be described as vertical communication. It's threading a theme and message throughout the whole range of activities. For example, I worked on the state of the state address in Alabama. We started with a text. But that text also united with the visuals we had that night. We had a fourth grade class come in and sing the state song, which had never been done in Alabama because they don't let people on the floor. So they had to violate a lot of traditions to allow that. So you have Don Siegelman speaking about the future of education and he's basically pointing to the future of Alabama right there in the chamber, that is, the fourth-graders. So you've got the visual and the text, then you've got the agenda, which has been developed over time, both with focus groups and with polling, so there is a unification of message.

Even if you didn't hear the speech, the picture of the governor standing at the podium with a group of fourth graders singing in front of him reinforced what he had already run on, which was "Children are my priority and education is what we have to take care of."

There are three basic elements in communication. The most powerful, of course, is visual. The next substantial component in communication is tone, that is, the emotional tone(s) connected to any concept being communicated. Mehrabian's study concluded that tone makes up about 38 percent of a communicator's effectiveness.

- A song comes on the radio that suddenly "takes you back" to your high school days. Maybe even to a specific event. For a brief moment, you relive it in your imagination. You see it, smell it, taste it, and emotionally feel it.

- The smell of a stranger's perfume sends a sudden wave of emotion through you as your memory briefly takes you back to a past relationship.

- It is difficult to remember what you had for lunch three days ago, but easy to vividly recall an accident you had ten years ago as if it were yesterday—along with all of the feelings and emotions it caused!

As these examples illustrate, people tend to remember concepts when they are attached to emotions. As with visual images, when an individual experiences strong emotions, the brain locks on to those emotions as well and stockpiles them for future reference. These strong emotions are usually interwoven with events and all the senses (odor, sight, sound, taste, and touch) connected to those events. Later, if a similar sensation is experienced, the strong emotion connected to the original experience may be brought to the forefront of your consciousness once again. Because that strong emotion was interwoven with a past event, not only is the emotion relived but many of the associated elements may also be re-experienced. For example:

As a child, you loved banana-flavored "slushees" from the neighborhood convenience store. Twenty years later, you try a banana daiquiri for the first time and the initial taste brings back fond memories of your bike-ride visits to that little corner market with your friends. You vividly remember the hot days, reading comic books off the rack, giggling at the store owner's frustration with your loitering, and stuffing your mouth full of Bazooka bubble gum. A fleeting rush of memories, all from one taste of a daiquiri. Of course, after finishing that daiquiri, along with a few more, you forget all about the convenience store, along with the names of your friends, family, and where you parked your car.

Madison Avenue has perfected the concept of using emotional tones to persuade potential customers. Ad agencies know that the average American is bombarded with something like 1,400 advertisements and messages each day, making it almost impossible to grab anyone's attention without attaching emotional tones to their products. Recently a television commercial featured a man and a woman who happen to get into the same elevator. As they ride the lift in silence, the television viewer is privy to their innermost thoughts. During the brief time these strangers are together, they fantasize about one another. Each imagines a first kiss with the other on a first date, then intertwined in a beautiful wedding ceremony, and finally having children. The elevator ride comes to a stop, the doors open, and the two part ways without a single word. Can you guess what the commercial advertised? Wedding rings? Nope. Family planning? I think not. The commercial was for jeans. *Jeans*! The advertisement didn't promise a great fit or long-lasting wear. It was designed to grab attention by impinging on the strongest of human emotions. The next day, as I rode the elevator to my office floor, what do you think popped into my head? Wedding rings? I don't think so.

For the most part, advertisers don't stress the product. They focus on the emotional benefits that might be enjoyed by the purchaser—social advancement, sexual gratification, wealth, etc.—powerful emotional elements that have been experienced by the viewer previously, now being tapped and re-wrapped around the present concept of the product. The next time you ride an elevator, maybe you'll think about jeans, too!

Communication without emotional tone is flat and uninteresting. More to the point, it isn't human. In fact, it's almost impossible to communicate without the auditor comprehending an attached tone—even if tone is unintended by the communicator. That's the interesting thing about human beings: we are not satisfied with nothingness; we will not accept a void. Presented with empty space, we'll fill it with something. I'm reminded of this every time my wife and I move into a new home. I won't move until she promises me the closet space in the new house is more than adequate. And it usually is. For about six months. Until we can find a new home with even more closet space.

In the 1940s, Sergei Eisenstein did an interesting study demonstrating the viewer's tendency to fill tonal voids. A Soviet film director who pioneered the use of the montage, and one of the most influential film technicians of his time, Eisenstein took still photographs of subjects who were asked not to show any emotion during their photo sessions. When these pictures were shown, viewers would inevitably assign emotions to the subjects in each picture. Eisenstein would then crosscut pictures of different objects, and show them to a new set of viewers who would then assign completely different emotions to the pictured subjects.

For example, viewers were shown a series of pictures featuring different kinds of people, and asked to give an impression of each image. They would usually assign emotional tones such as: "The old man is angry," "The little girl is pensive," and "The old woman is tired."

Another set of viewers was shown the same series of images, this time crosscut with pictures of inanimate objects. Before seeing the old man the viewer might see a picture of an apple, before the old woman, a picture of a valentine, and before the little girl, a picture of a rag doll. This second group of viewers would usually assign different emotions than the first set of viewers, i.e., the old man is hungry, the little girl is lonely and the old woman is in love.

When a communicator realizes that his audience will assign emotional tones where none exist and that his choice of emotional tones is just as important as his choice of words, the ability to use what's needed in different situations and to eliminate what's unnecessary becomes a real asset.

Bob Goen: I'm not sure if I really had an epiphany one day about the use of emotional tones. It just made sense to me. The guy that I always looked up to and patterned myself after was Dick Clark. Dick wasn't a "star." He wasn't an "untouchable." He just seemed like the kind of guy who was doing a show because that's just what he did. And he seemed like the kind of guy who would be approachable if you saw him on the street. I see that as a positive thing.

I really think Dick is somebody worth emulating because he's always been easy and likable with no flash. He is just the guy you can talk to and believe in and understand and relate to. So that's always the way I've pointed. I don't think it's something he's having to force. I think it is a part of him, but I don't think it is the only part of him. With me, I think it's a much higher percentage of who I am than who he is. He's also a producer. And as you know, to be a producer, you've got to have much tougher areas to your personality. So he's got that. But he's able to click it on and off when needed. Wearing different hats takes different skills and different parts of one's core and the skill to turn them on and off when needed.

The master understands the power of weaving emotional tones throughout his craft. Thus, the next maxim of communication:

MAXIM #2

The second most powerful element
in communication is **Emotional Tone**.

To illustrate the power of emotional tone, let's take a look at the sentence,
"I never said I thought you were crazy."
In and of itself, the sentence doesn't mean anything. But if we stress or "punch" just one word, by placing a bit more volume on it than any other, the sentence will take on a very specific meaning. Saying...

I never said I thought you were crazy. ...may very well imply that others do, in fact, think you are crazy. Saying...

I *never* said I thought you were crazy. ...states emphatic denial.

Saying... I never *said* I thought you were crazy. ...tells you, not only do I think you're insane, I've probably written about it. And so on. If we were to continue this exercise, stressing each individual word, we would end up with at least eight different meanings that could be attributed to this one sentence. The next step is to add emotional tone to the mix. In Chapter 4, on *Quality Core*, we found that an individual's core encompasses all human emotions.

Quickly now, name a few emotions you have in your core.

Whenever I suggest this during a coaching session, the response is usually something like, "Love, hate, happy, and sad." And that's great for starters. But as a communicator on the road to mastery, one must be aware of all options. As they say, "Knowledge is power!" So, how many emotions are actually in your core? Let's see if we can't expand the list just a bit. I'll take three minutes and jot down the first ones that come to mind.

– Exhausted – Angry – Confused – Ecstatic – Guilty – Suspicious
– Hopeful – Lonely – Love-struck – Hysterical – Frustrated – Over-whelmed – Confident – Smug – Sad – Mischievous – Disgusted – Embarrassed
– Jealous – Bored – Anxious – Frigid – Enraged – Ashamed
– Cautious – Depressed – Surprised – Shocked – Shy – Puppy love

Not bad for three minutes. Think about each of the emotions listed. Each is unique in its own fashion. At some point, it would be a wonderful exercise for you to continue the process, adding to the list and thinking about each individual emotion and how it manifests itself within your core. The more familiar you are with your tools, the more accessible they become. And the stronger your ability will be to utilize them.

Back to the original question, "How many emotions are actually in your core?" The answer is: "I have no earthly idea!" Hundreds? Thousands? Got to be a lot. Let's take an emotion and add it to our original sentence:

If I snicker while saying… *I* never said I thought you were crazy … the tone becomes derogatory in a malicious, superior way. And the implication may very well be that I lead the bandwagon in thinking you are a loon. On the other hand, if I yell while saying the same sentence, stressing the exact same word, the tone becomes angry and the message becomes quite different: clearly upset that you would even question my loyalty.

EXERCISE # IO:

Choose a word to stress in the phrase "**I never said I thought you were crazy**," adding an emotion from the list above. Say the phrase out loud, stressing the word and emotion you chose. Think about the message that is actually being communicated when you say it in that fashion. Do the exercise again stressing the same word with a different emotion.

As the above activity illustrates, using two different emotions while stressing the same word communicates two completely different meanings. Assuming there are at least 100 emotions in your core, using 100 emotions while stressing just one word would give you at least 100 choices in deciding how to communicate the sentence. So how many ways can we communicate the phrase, "I never said I thought you were crazy?"

100	100	100	100	100	100	100	100	= 800
I	never	said	I	thought	you	were	crazy	

Using 100 emotions while stressing each individual word will give us as many choices as there are words in a sentence, multiplied by 100. If that isn't enough, consider the number of choices you have with an entire speech. We might as well try to calculate p (pi).

Bob Goen: Danny DeVito actually told me the story about his audition for *Taxi*. Apparently he had not been working all that much since he had done *One Flew Over the Cuckoo's Nest*. He's a short, squat guy. There're just not a lot of roles for a guy like that. So he knew that when the role of Louie came up, he would have to take the words in that script and make the character an over-the-top, aggressive, nasty, chip-on-his-shoulder kind of guy, despite what he looked like and despite his diminutive size.

So when he went to read for the part, the first thing he did was walk in the room, throw the script down on the casting director's desk and gruffly say, "Who wrote this s***?" And basically got the part based on that. Even though he eventually read, interpreting the lines based on that emotional tone, he knew from the first moment that he was going to get it.

He had to know exactly who the character was and what part of that character he could tap into. He found it in his inner core and put that out there. And that was it.

Thus, the third Maxim of Communication:

MAXIM #3

*There are as many ways to verbalize or interpret
a sentence as there are words in that sentence—
multiplied by 100!*

So what is left? If communication is 55 percent visual and 38 percent tonal, what is the remainder of the equation? What element makes up the remaining 7 percent? The answer is *text*. That is, the actual words of the concept: script, copy, sides, etc.

WORDS WITHOUT THOUGHTS

Getting back to Mehrabian's study, the breakdown of communication elements looks like this:

55% Visual
38% Tonal
7% Words
100% Communication

The concept that communicators should not rely on the words to drive their message is central to this discussion. That in fact, text means very little without the communicator's core wrapped around the idea breathing emotional life into the words. And consciously making the most interesting choices possible in style and delivery will render the whole experience more palatable and exhilarating.

If you are a writer, the "7% Words" portion of this formula could be a concept especially difficult to accept. Dick Christie is the perfect ex-ample. A Hollywood screenwriter whose last script recently sold for over $1,000,000, Dick's view of the written word is not uncommon among his peers:

> *Dick Christie:* I can tell you right off the bat that after having done all three, after having acted, written, and directed, after having seen everything from all different sides of the camera and all different sides of the stage, I can say with some personal authority that it's all in the page. Writers are the most important people in the business. Because if it's not on the page, you can't create it. You can't create something from nothing. And it's got to be there to begin with. Believe me, Lawrence Olivier could not have made a poorly written situation comedy good.

But remember we are not discussing the rudiments or merits of writing. Our subject is not the facets of forging a well-crafted newspaper column, script or novel. We are talking about the dynamics of communication for a *viewing and listening* audience, whether it be reporting or acting or giving a speech, in front of a camera or a live audience. And this is not to say words have no significance. I know Mehrabian's numbers seem harsh, but I have actually seen studies that say words make up only 1 percent of the communications equation. I use Mehrabian as an example because I love words. I love to read great literature. I love to write. And as an actor, I would certainly rather be involved with a project crafted by the likes of William Shakespeare, William Goldman or Stephen Sondheim than have to wade my way through *dreck*.

But consider this: Last year alone, Audience Research & Develop-ment[10] polled over 30,000 viewers on their likes and dislikes regarding local television newscasts. Of those individuals, not one ever uttered the phrase "I love the writing!" In fact, they almost always placed the suc-cess or failure of a news presentation directly on the shoulders of the mainline anchors and their delivery of the information.

Lucy Himstedt, WFIE-TV's general manager, agrees with those view-ers, as well as most of her industry's managers, when she describes the style of storytelling she wants from her anchors:

Lucy Himstedt: If you tell every story alike, who is listening to any of them? You've got to have some interpretation. That's not bias, that's interpretation. You have to interpret your copy in some fashion. Otherwise, if you're reading the story about the murder and reading the story about the new baby at the zoo, who's going to hear the difference? Charles Kuralt and Charles Osgood are dynamite storytellers. I love to listen to how they tell stories. They just say it. I think where people really get caught up is in the 'hard news' storytelling. They are afraid they'll sound melodramatic or biased. It amazes me that someone can tell a story about a whole lot of dead people and it sounds like a story about what happened on Wall Street today.

The initial reactions of most people who watch television, films, speeches, and theatre are usually in the same vein. Viewers tend not to consider the contribution of the writer, director, producer, et al., as significantly as that of the central communicator. If the presentation is wonderful or lousy, in their minds it is the communicator who made it so. Initial praise or criticism will most certainly always be funneled in that direction. As my first public speaking coach used to say, "A great storyteller can make a bad script sound good. But a great script will never save a bad storyteller!"

AUTHOR'S RANT - SUPPLEMENTAL

Waxing on about my love for great literature reminded me that not long ago I had a conversation with a sixteen-year-old producer's apprentice who didn't understand why the phrase "dial the phone" was in existence. She asked, in earnest, "Why don't they call it 'touch-tone' the phone?" As I explained the origin of dialing (harking back to the days of my youth, rotary phones and, apparently, dinosaurs), it occurred to me that this girl's life—filled with instant gratification, fast food and shopping malls—had never been enriched by in-depth study of any significant part of our country's history. This exemplifies a situation I have found most distressing in the past ten years. Many of my newer students/clients don't have the proper education to support their quest for success. They want to craft their own scripts but have never learned the fundamentals or the disciplines of writing. They want to choose their own material but have never studied the classics, so they find it hard to distinguish good from bad, depth from surface, classic from commercial.

A Master Communicator must be able to relate the Human Condition to others. Yet one can not relate what one does not understand. To relate the Human Condition, one must have one's own perspective on it. And perspective comes with living life as fully as possible, and studying everything one can not experience. Or mall shopping and eating "Happy Meals." Take your pick.

QUALITY KEYS

- *The First Maxim of Communication*: The most powerful element in communication is visual.

- *Master Communicators inspire their auditors to actually see the concepts being communicated*. Once visualized, the concepts become that much more powerful and enduring.

- *The Second Maxim of Communication*: Emotional tone is the second most powerful element in communication. Communication without emotional tone is flat and uninteresting. More to the point, it isn't human.

- *The Third Maxim of Communication*: There are as many ways to verbalize or interpret a sentence as there are words in that sentence, multiplied by 100!

- *Communicators should not rely on the words to drive their message*. Text means very little without the communicator's core wrapped around the idea; breathing emotional life into the words.

- *The Master Communicator relates the Human Condition by having perspective*. Perspective comes from living life as fully as possible and studying everything one can not experience.

6 THE HUMAN CONDITION

A LONE MAN, IN HIS FORTIES AND SEEMINGLY in good health, has a fatal heart attack while riding in an elevator. He dies suddenly and horribly alone. But the real tragedy of this story is the way in which the man's wife learns of his death. A policeman comes to the house, knocks, wedges a note describing the terrible event into the doorjamb, and then hops back into his patrol car and speeds away before she can answer the door.

Never happen, right? I wouldn't have thought so either, but this incident actually did occur. I know, because the woman in this story is a relative. But the point of telling you this story is not for me to engage your sympathy. It is for you to gauge your own reaction.

You see, when I relate this story at seminars, those in attendance always gasp in unison at realizing the wife must learn of her husband's death from reading a scribbled note. I then act astonished at the audience's response and want to know why they reacted in such an odd manner. After all, she did get the information, right? And the data is all that really matters, right?

The average person is usually horrified at the thought of receiving this kind of tragic information in such a cold and unfeeling manner.

Most people say they'd rather hear it from a cop than from a note. Better yet, they'd rather learn about it from a friend than from a cop. And the strongest preference would be to get the news from a family member instead of a friend. In fact, when receiving emotionally charged information, not only does it seem natural to want it from another human being, but also the closer the messenger is to the information, the more comfortable we are hearing it.

What the fascinating communicator understands is that for the most part, people are not interested in data, per se. People are interested in the emotional elements that connect them to those data. They relate to the information better, have more affinity for that information and will remember it longer when it is intertwined with the *Human Condition.*

The Human Condition: 1. The complex of fundamental human behavioral patterns, ideas and attitudes.

2. Those fundamental dispositions and traits susceptible to or representative of a human being's sympathies, passions, failings and triumphs.

3. The conscious understanding of good and evil, spirit and mortality.

Consider your personal notions regarding Human Condition. After winning a city marathon, would you rather receive your kudos by comparing scores on the tote board or by basking in the warmth of a cheering crowd? Would you rather find out you landed a great new job through a business letter or a congratulatory handshake from your new boss?

And what of imparting information? Would sending a birthday card be as effective as throwing a surprise party for your best friend? Both actions communicate the same sentiment. Which would be more appreciated? And which would be more self-satisfying?

And what of reading? How about putting on those fuzzy slippers, getting a cup of hot chocolate and settling in for the evening with a really good book on calculus. What? Not enough Human Condition for you? Well, there's always algebra! "If Frank left Los Angeles on a train traveling at 30 miles an hour, and Rita left Chicago on a bus traveling at 60 miles an hour, how long would it take before...you went insane from boredom?"

In each of these examples, the event is not as important to the partici-
pant as the Human Condition that can be derived from that event. Data
mean very little to people if not attached to the Human Condition. The
natural inclination is to gravitate toward experience within an event
that offers the strongest Human Condition available.

Bill Taylor is the chairman of the board of Media Advisors International (MAI), the largest strategic consulting, talent placement, talent
coaching, and custom research service in the world. MAI's clients include broadcast and cable networks, major television studios, television
syndicators, local television stations, newspapers, and publishers worldwide.
Having said all that, Bill Taylor's message to his clients about communication is pretty simple:

> *Bill Taylor:* Communication is imparting ideas. It's convincing some-
> one of something. And you have to be fairly persuasive to do that.
> Life's about persuasion. And many times it's about putting the other
> person first rather than yourself. Or finding benefits along the way.
> It's not something that, for most of us anyway, comes naturally.
>
> There are several elements that go into creating good communi-
> cation. First and foremost is knowledge. To give a speech you must
> have knowledge to impart—something important enough to say.
>
> Second is sincerity; speaking from the heart and having a passion
> for what you are talking about. Knowledge is driven by sincerity and
> the passion to enlighten or persuade somebody.
>
> The third would be speaking clearly. Speaking as people speak.
> Speakers so often don't use 'people words.' In everyday conversa-
> tion, people often talk in short bursts, short phrases. We don't talk
> in long convoluted sentences with commas and semicolons. Many
> speakers who write and then read their speeches don't deliver from
> the heart. Unfortunately, when they sit at a typewriter or computer,
> something happens between the brain and the fingers and the screen
> that makes it come out as prose rather than the kinds of words that
> people really understand. A good speaker communicates to his au-
> dience in people-speak.

Mr. Taylor states that the tenet of good communication is nothing fancy: instead you must know who you are talking to, know what you're talking about, say it plainly, and say it with sincerity. I would take that a step further, and suggest that one can not possibly do these things without hooking into the Human Condition. To know your audience demands an understanding of human behavior, ideas, and attitudes. To speak with genuineness is to dip from the well of human emotions.

And of course you remember our successful political advisor, Rick Dent. What does Rick advise his politicians to do when they want so badly to set out an agenda to the general public and potential voters?

> *Rick Dent:* It's so simple that I'm embarrassed to be talking about it. Look, voters have hard lives. They work nine-to-five, nine-to-six, nine-to-seven. Then they probably spend about an hour in traffic trying to get home. They've got kids, so first thing they've got to do is get dinner on the table. Then it's time to clean up the mess. Then the kids have to take a bath. Then they've got to put them bed and read them a story. Now it's 9:30 or ten o'clock. The last thing in the world they care about is politics or issue-related communications. If you are going to connect with those people, you've got to understand the lives that they're living, what's important to them. And you've got to communicate with them in a very simple fashion because they're preoccupied with more important things.

So even politicians need to concern themselves with communicating the Human Condition. Amazing! In fact, whether the communicator is a politician, general, news anchor or taxi driver, no matter the profession, no matter the message—The fourth maxim of communication:

MAXIM #4

People don't care about data.
What they care about is
The Human Condition!

Understanding this basic characteristic of human nature is significant to the Master Communicator. The ability to utilize that understanding
in communication is paramount.

MUZAK NEWZAK

Each year I work with at least 130 anchors and thirty reporters in twenty-
five local news stations across the country, ranging in market size from
top-ten to 200. As much as I attempt to approach every coaching situation as a fresh experience and every individual as unique, there is one
malady that seems to plague many broadcasters and must constantly be
addressed across the board: It is the tendency to whitewash delivery. It
is the fear of sounding biased, which has forced many of these anchors
and reporters into reading their scripts with as little tonal variation as
possible. At times their on-air presentation becomes so pedantic one
wonders how it became news in the first place. And it is that placid,
singsong delivery that turns viewers off, along with their TV sets.

> *Bill Taylor:* The problem with local television is that it's a factory.
> While those who work in the news department are mostly college
> graduates and wear white shirts, they might as well be blue collars
> carrying lunch buckets, because they are going to the factory and
> producing the same little widgets on the same assembly line every
> day. You can compare reporter packages done in the field, one after
> the other, and they are all formulas. They are all the same, written
> in the same fashion with sound-bites showing up in the same way.
> Oh, there are rarities, and they are the ones we pay attention to:
> "Wow, is that different. Is that person good!"
>
> The same can be said for the anchors, weathercasters and sports-
> casters. It's all formula. It's been a factory all day long, so there's little
> opportunity for them to be great communicators. The viewer's affin-
> ity for them isn't based so much on their great communication skills
> as it is simply tenure and frequency in that chair. We tend to like
> them, even trust them, because they are there every night. But the
> limits on great communications are enormous because of the factory
> mentality of television. And that speaks to network television as

well. Anything that falls outside that realm is "tainted journalism." And it is this factory mentality that will be the demise of local television news and even the network news, because people can now get information, serious information, in so many different ways. From the people who can communicate that information well, whether it be the Rush Limbaughs or the Paul Harveys, to shows such as *Entertainment Tonight, Inside Edition, Dateline* and *20/20*.

How a story will be told to convey the Human Condition should be of paramount concern to the broadcaster. For years, viewers in model audience groups[11] have overwhelmingly agreed that the mere "facts" of a fire, a flood, a shooting, or the national debt are not enough to hold their interest. They hear about fires, floods, shootings, and debts every day, and quite frankly the statistics become numbing after awhile.

Bill Taylor: Those broadcasters who don't want to communicate with the Human Condition because they are afraid of "tainting the truth" should be selling shoes. It's wrong. That's all I can say. They used to say, "But look at the network news." Look closely at the network news. Listen closely to the way they write and present the news. Yes, Peter Jennings and Ted Koppel are personalities and have a certain mystique to them, but both of those guys are extremely good communicators and they use most of the reportorial elements to tell stories. So you can't use those guys as your "I'm gonna hang my hat on that 'cause we need to sound professional." That doesn't work anymore. You can't use PBS. Listen to *All Things Considered*. It uses every element. You talk about people-speak. You talk about creative writing. You talk about music. At the beginning of a piece you may hear sounds, maybe the sound of the rushing river. And then you hear someone saying "Sally Mae Joe, a single mother of two, lives in a small shack along the bubbling waters of this river..." and all of a sudden in that moment you have a visual description and you know this person. Hell, we don't do that in television. We don't even let the visuals do that in television. We get in the way of the visuals, we get in the way of the words, we get in the way of everything.

So if anyone gets out of school thinking that that's professional, that's about the most unprofessional thing you can do is not be a communicator. We're here to tell a yarn. We're here to tell a story. Now the story should be factual. Not objective. There's no such thing as objectivity. It should be balanced. We should have balanced views in a story. Because nobody's objective, given who we are as human beings. But we can do balance. Not both sides, because there're more than two sides. There are many sides. And many stories need to balance out the issues at hand. That's fair. That's good journalism. But to be dry, to be unemotional, to be detached, that's someone better suited to selling shoes.

What is important to the viewer is the Human Condition. What of the people involved? It isn't news without human impact. As one viewer put it:

Television Viewer: So we're a trillion dollars in debt. So what? I've never seen a trillion of anything. Those numbers mean nothing to me. Help me to feel that a lot of people in my community may be out of a job because we're a trillion dollars in debt. Then I'm interested. That's information I value. That's news!

Flash In the Pan

The explosive, rapid expansion of satellite, cable, video rentals, and worldwide distribution has created a global market ravenous for a continuous stream of "product." The entertainment industry, in its frenzied desire to feed its golden goose, continues each year to churn out an ever-greater number of films and television shows that seem to come and go faster than campaign promises after election day.

At first glance, the few films and television projects that do rise to the surface of our collective consciousness and remain a part of our pop-culture don't seem to have much in common. Just take a look at the "Best Picture" Oscar winners for a period of ten years:

OSCARS FOR "BEST PICTURE"
1999 *American Beauty*
1998 *Shakespeare in Love*
1997 *Titanic*
1996 *The English Patient*
1995 *Braveheart*
1994 *Forrest Gump*
1993 *Schindler's List*
1992 *Unforgiven*
1991 *Silence of the Lambs*
1990 *Dances with Wolves*

Choosing a few at random, *Schindler's List* is the story of a Catholic factory owner who saves the lives of hundreds of Polish Jews from the Nazis. *Braveheart* is a 13th-century epic tale of a Scottish rebel warrior. *Forrest Gump* is about a dimwitted, good-natured person who floats through life. And *Unforgiven* is a western that follows an old gunslinger as he is forced out of retirement for one last job. If we were to continue with the rest of the list, we would find that each film is completely different from the next. Plots, dramatic styles, time periods, geographical locations, subject matter, characters, even the starring actors. Different, different, different, different and different! So how does a studio know what scripts should be produced? And what films will be the winners? One Hollywood executive told me:

Executive Producer: Trying to predict the success of a film is like trying to choose the best passenger seat on a dirigible. You may be the best seat-picker in the business, but if you're flying on the Hindenburg, it makes no difference. And there's no way to know if you're on the Hindenburg until you've burned to the ground.

You may argue that using a list of Oscar winners for this discussion really isn't fair because they are chosen by the Academy of Motion Picture Arts and Sciences members and don't reflect the tastes of the general public. So as not to be elitist, let's take a quick look at the top ten highest-grossing movies of all time:

Highest-Grossing Movies of All Time
Domestic gross ticket receipts in millions
(as of June 2000)

1.	$601	*Titanic*	1997
2.	$461	*Star Wars*	1993
3.	$431	*Star Wars: The Phantom Menace*	1996
4.	$400	*E.T.*	1977
5.	$357	*Jurassic Park*	1994
6.	$330	*Forrest Gump*	1982
7.	$313	*Lion King*	1994
8.	$307	*Return of the Jedi*	1997
9.	$306	*Independence Day*	1997
10.	$293	*The Sixth Sense*	1998

Quite a different list! And, by the looks of it, the general public's taste is a bit more consistent than the Academy's. Here, the highest grossing films seem to be fantasy-based and/or action-driven. But is that enough to ensure that people will want to see a film? For that answer just ask the producers of *King Solomon's Mines* (1985), *Surf Ninjas* (1993) or *Waterworld* (1995), three fantasy-based, action-driven movies that bombed at the box-office.

The fact is, nobody can predict a hit. But there is one way to hedge the bet, one element that you will find in every film on both top-ten lists, one dynamic that every audience member can relate to, no matter what the subject matter, no matter what the genre: That dynamic is the Human Condition. Usually found in relationships.

Yes, we loved the action sequences and pyrotechnics in *Star Wars*, but what we fondly remember are the relationships between the characters of Luke Skywalker, Han Solo, and Princess Leia. Yes, the search for a serial killer can be fascinating in and of itself, but what compels us in *Silence of the Lambs* is the relationship between the determined FBI trainee, Clarice Starling, and the brilliant psychotic criminal, Hannibal Lecter.

To the viewer, conveying the Human Condition would seem to be the sole responsibility of the actor. But if you were to ask the professionals who work behind the scenes, most would disagree. Directors, producers, editors, camera operators, even the craft services people would insist that they too play a part in helping the project convey the Human Condition. And they would be right. David Semel is one such individual. A very talented director who has worked extensively in television episodics, situation comedies, commercials, and music videos, David's current credits include multiple episodes of *Beverly Hills 90210*, *Party of Five*, *Buffy the Vampire Slayer*, *Malibu Shores*, *Seventh Heaven*, and the comedy series *Duet* and *Open House*. His view on the Human Condition:

David Semel: I have been doing this since I was a kid, and I have always loved editing and the visual. I love photography and design. My mother is an interior designer. Yet, I don't think anyone goes to a movie and walks out saying, "I hated those actors, but weren't those sets gorgeous?" To me, all that stuff supports the humanity coming out of the characters. I find myself stressing that there has got to be a reality, truth, and a heart to the character. Something the viewer can connect with. I want the audience to connect.

That identification comes from shared experiences. It is the ability to say either, "Yeah that has happened to me before and I reacted that way," or "If I were in that situation, how would I react?" If you set up a character a certain way and there is something about that character that is endearing or attractive or alluring, that is why people go to the movies. They will go on the trip with you as long as there is a reality and a truth and a through-line.

Now as a director, I see an actor using his core to find the Human Condition as being a good thing. It is a bad thing if it relates to being a "star." Take, for example, Arnold Schwarzenegger. He is obviously doing something right because people love that stuff. But it is about seeing Arnold Schwarzenegger in those roles. More power to him. It doesn't interest me as much. I actually hate those movies. I would rather see an actor who is going to bring the core of a Jack Nicholson. The core doesn't change, but what Nicholson does with it in every movie allows him to be a navy base commander in one and the devil in the next. The core is the truth that he brings to the role and the humanity he brings. It gives me something to connect to. I'm just not turned on by that star-driven crap.

When creating or deciding on a project, the questions all writers, actors, directors and executive producers should ask themselves are, "Are there faceted relationships? Are there relationships we care about? Does this project center around and highlight the Human Condition?" As my granddaddy used to say, "Flash without substance is just a flash in the pan!"

EXERCISE #11

(You'll need paper and pencil for this.)

List five films, television shows and/or plays you've enjoyed recently. Beside each one, write down a human condition element that gave the project substance.

"LISTEN, CHUCK..."

There is a wonderful (probably apocryphal) Hollywood "actor's story" about Charlton Heston. Very early in his career, a very young Heston landed the lead role in *Ben-Hur*, one of the biggest film epics of all time. *Ben-Hur* also happened to be a huge production nightmare, even by today's standards. Plagued with thousands of extras, budget problems, schedule concerns, technical obstacles, clashing on-set personalities, and time constraints, the process was not the most conducive to an actor's creativity. On top of everything else, Heston felt an extra weight of responsibility upon his shoulders because he was the lead character.

After a couple weeks of filming, the director, an anxious William Wyler, quickly marched up to Heston, studied him for a moment and haltingly said, "Listen, Chuck, could you...uh, well...act better?" Wyler took another beat trying to formulate a more constructive suggestion, but then shook his head and shrugged his shoulders. Before the stunned Heston could respond, Wyler spun around and bee-lined away to jump his next production hurdle. Of course, Wyler's terse bit of advice only added to Heston's anxiety, and, for a short time "Chuck's" acting became even worse.

Things obviously worked out for the best since Charlton Heston ultimately won an Oscar for that performance; but this story points up a common problem that happens all too often with communicators in every field. It is easy for a director, producer, writer, news director, general manager, or agent, to suggest results. We all know what we like when we see it. William Wyler knew what "good acting" looked like. It's easy to suggest creative excellence. On the other hand, explaining to someone *how to achieve* creative excellence is not so easy. Many people in positions of power who attempt to do so just don't know how. And so the communicator spends a lifetime hearing cryptic comments like, "Could you give it a bit more energy, please?" or "Could you find a more exciting choice there?" "Could you act better?"

And the acquiescent communicator backs away, smiling and nodding, while thinking to himself, *Act better? What the heck does this guy mean, 'Act better?' Tell me something I don't know! Energy? Energy this, pal! Hey, I got a choice for ya'! Right here with your choice!* Smile and nod, smile and nod.

David Semel: One of the elements that reality and truth are based on is humor. Laughter is a release of tension. That's a big reason why people go to films. It is a great way to emotionally lead an audience. If you can get them laughing, it leaves them completely unsuspecting for whatever else you want to throw at them. I bring that with me everywhere I go. I like to bring it on the set. You work these kinds of hours and under this kind of pressure, you might as well be having fun. It translates up on the screen. Laughing is infectious, just as yawning is.

I care about everybody on the set. I'm not Mother Theresa, but I'm concerned with everybody. It is my responsibility to make sure everybody on that set is getting their creative input. I don't think an actor is any different from a grip. Everybody should be afforded the same courtesy and human decency. Myself included.

The difference with actors is that what they are doing is so personal. Directors of photography, or directors, or costume designers, or production designers can point to something tangible and say, "That is my work," and distance themselves. But actors can't. So when I offer criticism to actors, I try to focus on all the positives. On the set, when it comes to doing anything I can to make them feel comfortable and able to do their work, that is my chief focus. I will stay up all night, and I will think things through a million times to try to convey whatever I'm trying to say in a shot or a camera angle, but I still believe ultimately that an actor is giving above and beyond what the audience is hooking into.

So the Human Condition comes from everything. What the actor brings. What an actor is wearing tells you a lot about the humanity. The way an actor appears and the lighting on an actor—everything is contributive. You can't sit around and say, "Okay, an actor contributes 60 percent and the crew contributes 20 percent." Who cares about those numbers? What is important, as a director, is that as long as everybody is coming at it in the same way, then it all comes together. If everybody is off doing his own thing, it doesn't come together. As a director, one of the main concerns is to make sure that it all fits in the big picture. Sometimes you go see a film, and it is like the actors are in their own totally different movie.

CORE WRAP

So far we've discovered that the interjection of Human Condition is a key element in the communicator's creative excellence. And to have Human Condition, communicators must wrap their core qualities around the message, around their work, and around their craft.

Now, I know what you're thinking. *Wrap my core? What the heck does this guy mean, 'wrap my core?' Wrap this, pal!* Smile and nod, smile and nod.

And so, the question arises: "How?" How does one wrap one's core around anything? So far, if we were to create a paradigm for fascinating communication, it would look something like this:

Message → ??? → Quality Core → Human Condition → Communicate

Communication begins with the raw material or the message. Then somehow the fascinating communicator must wrap his *quality core* around that material. Once done, that core will automatically support the material with the *Human Condition*, which then becomes a foundation for the communicator to texture his craft by making exciting "choices."

So what is the missing link? What is the magic something that intertwines quality core with the message? To answer that question, let's first take a quick look at the word *energy*. If you have any history as a professional communicator, at some point in your career you've gotten the "note" from a director, producer, or critic that what you need is "Energy!" "Pick it up!" "More energy, please!" *"Energy!"* Smile and nod, smile and nod.

What is meant by this catchall phrase? When you think of *energy*, what comes to mind? What are all the adjectives or elements you can imagine "they" must mean when "they" bark out the demand, "More energy, please!" What does *energy* mean to you? What elements comprise *energy*?

Eventually, I ask all my clients to list their concepts of energy. Some of the answers I've gotten over the years are:

ENERGY =	Loud	Fast	Bubbly	Animation
	Vigor	Intense	Frenetic	Facial Expressions
	Liveliness	Pace	Dynamic	Vivacity
	Enduring	Orgasmic	Urgency	Happy
	Up	Excitement	Fun	mc2

I submit to you that although these answers are all correct, they are all results. One can create any of these states with energy. But the question remains "Where does the energy come from?" What actually forms energy? What gives one the power to tap into one's core qualities?

SITUATION:

You run out of a burning building, fervently searching for a fire fighter to help you save a child caught in that building. You find a fireman, rush up to him, grab his arms, look into his eyes, and before you utter a single word you think to yourself, "Hmm, the elements I think I'll choose for this situation are volume, vigor, pace, animation..."

I don't think so. You wouldn't think twice. You'd come at the guy without the slightest thought of choosing the right emotions, facial expressions, or body language, and fervently get your point across perfectly. The reason? You are *invested* in the situation. It *means* something to you.

When someone is invested in a situation or invested in a message, his core naturally wraps itself around that message. It is human nature.

SITUATION:

There's a knock at your front door. You open it to see Dick Clark and Ed McMahon standing there with a Publishers Clearinghouse Sweepstakes check made out in your name for a million dollars. Before you utter a single word, you remind yourself to have "pace, vivacity, orgasmic..."

I don't think so! You go crazy! You cry. You scream. You kiss Ed. Your core automatically wraps itself around the situation because you are *invested*. And there isn't a whole lot you can do about it. You're embarrassed about the sudden intimacy with Ed, but you just couldn't help it. Human nature. The fifth maxim of communication:

MAXIM #5

Energy = Investment

So the completed paradigm for fascinating communication looks like this:

Message → *Investment* → *Quality Core* →
Human Condition → *Communicate*

Energy can mean a lot of things that aren't necessarily "excitement." I remember being a pretty frenetic child. If Ritalin had been in vogue at the time, Mom would have hooked me up to a permanent intravenous drip. My running around department stores, generally creating havoc while she tried to shop, drove her crazy. She would plead with me to stop, constantly suggesting she was a heartbeat away from a "conniption fit." (Being a curious youth, the mere thought that I might witness what promised to be a pretty neat seizure actually fueled my kinetic nature.) My father, on the other hand, was not a "pleader." His energy manifested itself in a short, high-pitched whistle to get my attention, and then a quiet burning stare with eyes he apparently borrowed from a psychotic killer. My father's devotion to my mother, his total investment in that special relationship, created an energy that allowed him to pull primal survival elements from his core that wrapped themselves around his message to me. That one look told me exactly what it meant to him that I stop my "shenanigans." Deep, dark, and chilling. He was extremely invested! That was energy I'll never forget. I still get cold sweats whenever I walk through Sears.

Be Invested

The Master Communicator knows everything there is to know about his craft and the project(s) he is involved with. "Knowledge is power!" The more one knows and understands, the more potential there is for investment. Vahan Moosekian describes his notion of the fascinating communicator:

Vahan Moosekian: The most interesting actors, anchors, writers...the most engaging communicators of any kind, are the ones who live and observe life. To be an original, you have to like life, like people and have experiences. With the great directors of the past, movies hadn't been invented yet, so they all did other things. They were oil drillers, cooks on tuna boats, literary professors...they came from all walks of life.

Those who have hobbies and life experiences, raise kids and take them seriously...those are the people who are interesting to watch. Study your craft and know your profession. You wouldn't want to be with a doctor who wasn't up on medical procedures. I don't like communicators who are not up on their craft. They should do a lot of reading, study art, or do a lot in life.

A communicator must experience life. If he is going to be good, he must be a student of life.

For the actor, *investment* means continuous study of craft and complete involvement in current projects, no matter how small the part. Always seeking new and different techniques to work on various roles and on oneself. Constantly reading and learning about current and historical events. Being familiar with all forms of art and literature. Constantly enriching the soul.

Too often, beginning actors will only concern themselves with the particulars of whatever role they happen to be involved with at the moment, not taking the time to really understand the other characters in the piece, much less what the entire project is attempting to communicate.

David Semel: I like actors who bring very specific choices. A willingness to explore and try things and put themselves at risk. I know a lot of that comes from my creating a situation where they feel comfortable doing that. A lot of that comes from them trusting me. A lot of why I took your acting class was because even though I had spent all my time learning about editing and writing, I found it important that actors think and feel that I know what they are going through. And that I can create an environment where they are able to do their work.

An actor's preparation is extremely important. I don't like stupid actors. Everybody should do their homework. I don't expect actors to look at the bigger picture, but I also don't expect them to be out there just thinking of themselves. They should have a greater sense of where their character came from and where their character is going. They should have an understanding of what the movie is about. I get tons of things from actors. Sometimes I feel like I am an editor for actors. They bring me things. "Okay here is the big picture. Come back with specifics." They will bring me ideas about the character or a scene. We then decide if we should do that or not.

I don't think that I have—and I hope I never do—enough confidence that I can just dictate what everybody should be doing. I like to look at all the possibilities. I'll think things through so damn specifically and have a specific approach to something. I would like everyone around me to do that. At the same time, I am also open to everyone's interpretation. It just betters mine, if I'm smart enough to pick from other people. It reflects my approach to the material. Who knows what you are going to come up with in the end. Acting is all about doing your homework, thinking things through, having ideas and being willing to change and try other things.

Being invested means fully understanding all the characters, all the relationships, why the piece is structured in its fashion, why it was written, its dramatic style, what other styles the piece relates to, what the piece is trying to say, what the writer wanted to say, what the director is trying to communicate, what all the characters are struggling to accomplish, and on and on and on.

For the anchor, *investment* means taking ownership of every piece of copy being read. It is not enough to be a good reader. Viewers should have a sense that the anchor knows the subject intimately. The ability to completely involve oneself in a news piece, even unusual stories that come across the wire, takes more than a good speaking voice and great camera presence. The anchor must have a broad knowledge of world history and current events and be deeply immersed in local and regional concerns to be able to have and communicate perspective.

Bill Taylor: If there's one message I would give to a student in high school or college it is that in any business you have to have a lot of general knowledge about the world as well as a lot of specific knowledge about your specialty. Take the news business for instance. How can you interview and talk to economists or politicians or world affairs leaders if you don't know geography or history? It's amazing how many people show up to newsroom in the morning for a story conference and haven't even read the paper. They haven't listened to a radio newscast, they didn't see their morning newscast, they didn't watch CNN, they didn't do any of the things you should do to prepare your mind to go to work. To be successful in business you have to come prepared to work. And in preparing to work, for a newsperson, a journalist, you've got to simply be aware. You have to read, you have to listen. I know there's so much input coming in, but you've got to be able to understand who these people are in the news, and where they come from, and what they represent, and their viewpoints.

We've experimented with news stations over the years and found that you can collect a station's scripts for a week, develop a twenty-five-question current affairs test, and most people in the newsroom will flunk it. These are questions developed from their own newscasts, not something out of *Newsweek* or some textbook. It's the stuff they put on television and they don't even get it. It's been proven time and again. So what does that say about where we are? How unfortunate that is.

It's all about brainpower. The difference between one television newsroom and another has little to do with their physical facilities or their equipment, their satellite trucks, their live cameras, number of crews, etc. Each army in a town is usually equipped about the same. The only difference is the gray matter between their ears. How they use their brains. How they use their resources. How they think about the news. And frankly there's not enough thinking going on in most television newsrooms. They don't think about what they should really be covering, what is really important and how to dedicate their resources.

It is difficult to communicate perspective without having perspective. And make no mistake about it: viewers do not watch a particular local newscast on a particular station simply for the data. Most viewers assume they can get the bulk of that data anywhere, i.e., the newspaper, radio, the Internet, other newscasts, other stations. They watch a particular station and a particular anchor because they feel that is where they will get the best understanding of the relationship of current news elements, how those news elements relate to each other, how they relate to the world and, especially, how they personally relate to the viewer. That is perspective. In the viewer's mind, communicating that perspective is the anchor's job.

HARD WRAP

Energy potential and the ability to wrap core qualities around communication are directly related to the investment a communicator has with the material—pure and simple. If you really care about it, if it impacts your being in a significant fashion, the qualities that are most related will generally come to the forefront of your core. It is human nature.

Tom Amundsen: The worst moment in my career was on a sitcom when one of the leads after a whole week didn't know his lines. And we were in front of the audience. We kept having to go back and tape things again. We went through two scenes and he was making things up and it was awful. I actually went backstage and I asked him what was so important in his life that would cause him not to have the time to memorize the script for the show that gave him everything he has in his life. He had no answer.

Now the real problem was that he wasn't an actor. If you ever write a pilot for a network and they suggest that you cast a specific person, you smile at them and say, "What a great idea!" But if that happens and you're saddled with that person, then surround him with actors. Surround the show with people who are trained or who come from a theater background because those people know their work. They know the rules and they know the game. I don't care if they've done just two years of community theater, let alone fifteen years of regional theater and five years of Broadway. It's all about discipline. You surround whoever it is with these kinds of people and your life is going to be easier, because theatre trained actors don't forget where they've come from and what they've had to go through to get where they are. They don't necessarily feel that they deserve it like others do when they've been given a TV show or movie. Theatrically trained actors might feel that they have *earned* it. And that is a big difference.

It sounds like an old cliché, but do the work wherever you can find it. Whether it's in an old twelve-seat theater where people bring furniture from home so they can put on a play, or if it's at the Mark Taper Forum or the Guthery Theater. Just do the work because that is the only thing that trains you. Taking acting class is good, too.

Television is a personality-driven business. If you persist you may not be the star of the series but you'll probably work pretty consistently. Writers and producers don't have a lot of imagination and they tend to go to casting sessions with blinders on. They think they know who that character is. If you fit that, then boom, you are home free. It is a sad commentary but 90 percent of the decision is made when the actor walks through the door.

Now the only way to fight that is to be trained. Once you know how to act, you know how to read the signs, then you might be able to put the cherry on top of the sundae. Who are they going to go with, somebody who looks like the idea of what they are doing and is a good actor or somebody who just looks like who they think it should be? Since 90 percent of the decision is made when you walk through that door, if you are really good and really funny and know what you are doing, you can win that 10 percent and get the job. I've seen it happen.

I have also seen the guy who comes in and is not at all what they pictured but is wonderful and funny and such a good actor that he gets the job. That's what I mean about being prepared. Keep doing plays and keep up with acting classes. Like anything else, you can get rusty.

I am a firm believer in the fact that you can not teach someone to be funny or to act or to write. Those are all inherent talents. Taking classes and doing plays can bring out talent and refine it, but if you don't have it, you are never going to have it. If you don't have a sense of humor, you are not going to wake up one morning and say, "I know how to be funny!" That is why I have always said, "Surround yourself with trained actors because that is what will make your show a success!"

The best communicators care deeply about the material they are communicating. So much so that at times their fervor transcends ego. The communication and craft are so important that the message becomes more important than the messenger. Lesser communicators might not want to involve themselves, or shy away from complete involvement because they feel their credibility is at stake. The Master Communicator understands that credibility is easily lost if the auditor senses "flash without substance." Therefore, if a communicator decides to take on a project, the investment should be total and deeply rooted, without concern for adulation.

QUALITY KEYS

- *People don't care about data.* Data means very little to people if not attached to the complex of fundamental human behavioral patterns, ideas and attitudes. What people really care about is the Human Condition.

- *The Human Condition.* Those fundamental dispositions and traits susceptible to or representative of a human being's sympathies, passions, failings, and triumphs.

- *"Just the facts, ma'am."* Raw data is not enough to hold the news viewer's attention. They want perspective, and they want the Human Condition.

- *The common denominator in most successful films* is a strong portrayal of the Human Condition. This element can usually be found in character relationships.

- *Energy potential* and the ability to wrap core qualities around communication is directly related to the investment a communicator has with the material.

- *"Knowledge is Power."* Master Communicators seeks to know everything there is to know about their craft, their auditors and the world around them.

- *Investment for the actor* means continuous study of craft and complete involvement in all projects. Seeking new and different techniques to enhance the actor's process. Constantly reading and learning about current and historical events, being familiar with art and literature, constantly enriching the soul.

- *Investment for the anchor* means taking ownership of every piece of copy being read, having a broad knowledge of world history and current events, being deeply immersed in local and regional concerns, and always striving to communicate perspective.

■ THE GALLERY

DICK CLARK
in Times Square

RICK DENT, political advisor and Campaign Director
for Alabama Governor Don Siegelman

SHERI ALLEN
News Anchor for KTBS-TV

BILL TAYLOR, Chairman of the board
of Media Advisors International

GARY CHAPMAN, songwriter & host
of TNN's Prime Time Country

LUCY HIMSTEDT, General Manager of WFIE-TV
and MIKE BLAKE, news anchor

SANDRA CONNELL, President
of Talent Dynamics

BOB GOEN
host of *Entertainment Tonight*
photo by Charles Bush

ANNE WILKINSON
Talent Agent

LISA RINNA
star of *Melrose Place* and
2-time Soap Opera Digest Award winner
for *Days of Our Lives*

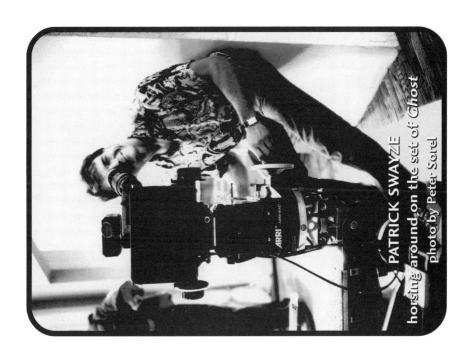

PATRICK SWAYZE
horsing around on the set of *Ghost*
photo by Peter Sorel

COACH GEORGE KARL
photo by Barry Gossage

7 THE ACTOR

AN EARLY CHILDHOOD MEMORY FINDS ME WAITING backstage for an entrance cue. Dressed in a goofy jester's outfit, trying to keep quiet the annoying jingle-bells attached in weird places all over my body, watching from the wings as the kid before me succumbs to stage fright and pees himself, center stage. It is here that I have my first taste of the actor's emotional cocktail: that sensory roller coaster of being scared to death of forgetting my lines (one line, actually), and exhilarated beyond belief that I am about to step into the limelight. And the moment following my big speech, when I hear that applause, I realize, at the ripe old age of six, that I am now a performance junkie. And I will be compelled over and over and for the rest of my life to seek that "fix" of fervent, rushing, conflicting emotions.

Ever since that critically acclaimed performance I have spent a good part of my life living and working with actors. And if the Chinese composition of the word is accurate, I would venture to say that every actor I've ever known was in a constant state of crisis. The last time I checked with the Screen Actor's Guild, there were about 84,000-plus members. They tell me over 80 percent of those thespians make less than $10,000 a year, and something like 30 percent receive no income at all.

From these statistics alone it is understandable why most actors are in the crisis mode. Pouring heart, soul and energies into a chosen profession while waiting tables to eke out a living and struggling for years with no guarantee of success can be spiritually draining.

And what of the 1 percent who make something like 40 percent of the available income? Recently I worked with a well-known personality who could buy and sell Beverly Hills a hundred times over. Actually, the executive producer called me to the set for "dialogue coaching." I quote the phrase because in the entertainment business this is often a euphemism for "star wrangling." As a matter of fact, over the years of visiting sets as a "dialogue coach," I can remember actually looking at a script in maybe two cases. Much of the time, the sessions are really meant as confidence builders to help a performer out of a slump (and his trailer) and back onto the set and to work.

In this instance, the actor was worried sick over an upcoming love scene. He considered his co-star "a ball-buster, along with the rest of Hollywood, damn it!" And he felt she was covertly upstaging him throughout the project. They weren't speaking to each other off the set, and he didn't know how to get through the sensitive love scene without strangling her. So he was just a tad worried about making it believable.

During that day, I also witnessed an argument with the director over the fear that his character was too weak, and a heated cell-phone conversation with his agent, regarding the lack of future possible quality projects; a sign his career might well be spiraling into oblivion. I did my part to get him through the scene without bloodshed, but it was interesting to note that this star's daily existence was not about the joy of having reached a high plateau of financial stability and leading roles. It was filled with battling his fears of *losing* those things, instead.

Now if you believe I'm telling tales out of school or, as one of my news anchor clients is fond of saying, "exaggerating the facts to the point of true lies," I would like to introduce you to Allan Katz. As a writer, producer and director, Allan's career spans decades and the gamut of entertainment media, including film, theatre, and literally hundreds of television shows. As a producer/writer, he garnered a Peabody Award and a Golden Globe nomination for *M*A*S*H**, and four Emmy nominations for *Cher*, *Laugh-In*, *M*A*S*H**, and *Rhoda*. Allan has also won an

Outer Circle Critics Award and a Drama Desk Award for his musical, *Song of Singapore*. Allan's executive producer credits include *The Fresh Prince of Bel Air*, *Blossom*, *Roseanne*, and *Charlie and Company*. He can also be credited with creating a number of situation comedies such as *The Goodbye Girl*, *Best Friends*, and *Charlie and Company*. So don't take my word for it. Listen to Allan:

Allen Katz: I did a short-lived series with Flip Wilson. He comes in early one morning, looks at the first couple of pages of the script, and before the morning read-through, he disappears. We can't find him for two or three days. His manager can't find him and he doesn't have an agent.

We finally locate him. He tells his manager that the script is "too herky-jerky" and that he is not going to do it. I don't know what he means by "too herky-jerky" because I've never had a discussion with him about the script. We waste another day trying to figure out "herky-jerky" because he won't come in and talk to me.

It turns out that in the teaser,[12] Flip's character is talking to his daughter and trying to watch television at the same time. Apparently, this is what Flip found to be a problem, it was "herky-jerky" to be doing two things at one time.

I said to his business manager, "Flip's reaction makes no sense to me. The teaser is two pages that has nothing to do with the story!" I ask about the rest of the script. The business manager tells me Flip is fine with the rest of the script.

"Tell Flip that we will do another opening if he is not comfortable with it!" The business manager says, "Okay."

Finally, Flip shows up. By now it is Wednesday and he says, "Okay I'm ready to go." No discussion about it. We shot the show on Friday with two less days of rehearsal and had to use cue cards. What the hell was that all about? All it did was make the show worse for no reason.

With Roseanne we had to throw out an entire script! But in that instance she was right. Part of the story paralleled her real life too closely, and what was going on in the trades and what was going on in the National Enquirer. She respectfully said, "I have a real problem doing this." She was going through a divorce and was having some problems with her kids, and the story paralleled too much of that. She just didn't want to do it so we threw it out. That happens. It made perfect sense and I respected her reasoning for wanting to do that. It means a lot more work. We had to send everybody home. We didn't have a script. We had to stay up all night long and come up with another story.

Just as the Chinese concept of crisis combines equal parts of danger and opportunity, it is important for the actor to keep a balanced perspective between the struggle for future goals and living in present time. There are hundreds of "Hollywood stories" like the ones above, which divulge the darker side of an actor's personality when faced with the daily struggles of life and career. On the other hand, there are just as many stories that reveal how masters not only relish their own journeys, but create situations along their way that enhance the journeys of those around them:

Allen Katz: My best experience in this business was working on *M*A*S*H*. It was the best because of a wonderful group of people and a wonderful concept. You could write and do anything you wanted with that show. You could do the worst word plays or you could do a poignant moment or you could do something that was meaningful and had some long-lasting value to it. You could even do the most foolish joke that made no sense at all. You could do them sometimes side by side. You had wonderful actors who took the material as if it were a Broadway stage play. They gave so much respect to the script and made everything work better than the words on the page. They respected the script and I respected them.

I'll give you one story about Alan Alda. Rarely if ever did he comment in any way about his problems with script. He always found a way to make everything work. It comes from his stage experience, where a script is a script and it is your job to do it. He would find the most remarkable ways to say ordinary lines that had to be delivered for the sake of information. Alan would do something with them to make them interesting in the same way that John Goodman did on *Roseanne*. John delivers all of the story, all the narrative stuff, and you think he is doing jokes. Or John will do it in such an interesting way that you won't be aware of it, but you are paying attention to everything he says. If it were some other actor, you would think he was reading the side of a *Crest* package.

Anyway, Alan came up to the office one day and said, "Look, I have a problem with something in the script that I would like to discuss with you."

Well, this sounded pretty serious. Especially because he rarely came up. He said, "In the script I have a relationship with one of the nurses."

I think it was Nurse Able. It was always either Able, Baker, or Charlie. He said, "I have no problem with the fact that I sleep with her in the script." It was a 'B' story, so the main story didn't have anything to do with their relationship.

Alan said, "My problem is, there is nothing in the script that indicates that I have any feelings for her as a human being. Not that I have to be in love with her or that there has to be a whole history. But something that says I care about her in some way or that we are just having this fling because we like each other. So, what I have done is written a couple of lines that make it better for me. Actually, I have written a couple of choices. If you don't like the lines and you want to write something else, I would really appreciate it. If you don't agree with me and you want me to do it the way it is, I will."

Now, this is *Alan Alda*, the star of the show, after five seasons. So what he tells me is that he has a problem, but he is not sure that I have the problem. He has come up with some alternatives. If I don't like the alternatives, but I agree that it is a problem, or that I want to serve him, then I can come up with some of my own. If I don't agree with the problem, he will willingly go right back down and do what is in the script.

I'll never forget it because it showed me the best way to do something like that. He didn't do it on the floor in front of everybody else. He didn't make an issue out of it. He didn't put the script down and say, "I'm not saying this!" or that "I have a big problem with this thing." None of that. It was the most and least manipulative thing that anybody could do.

I told him that we would do whatever he wanted. "We will rewrite it or we will use what you want!" Ultimately, I think we told Alan, "What you wrote is absolutely terrific, but we will come up with a few more choices and then you can pick and do whatever you want."

How could you not do that for him? Then you knew, when there was a problem, it was a real problem. When there wasn't, there wasn't. It rarely happened. It is not a testimonial to how good we were as writers. We were really good writers. It is a testament to actors, and how really good actors can find a way of doing things.

It is in our very nature to seek out new life-games to conquer. And many of us are constantly concerned with future "wins." But if our strivings for the next plateau are not balanced with a satisfaction for playing current games, the tastes of victory are bland, short lived and quickly forgotten. Traveling the road to mastery is understanding that *fervency of the journey is the goal*. For there is no Nirvana. And being fully invested in present-time activities is the real "win."

Therefore, the sixth maxim of communication:

MAXIM #6

Mastery is a fully invested
and fervent journey.
Mastery is not a destination.

NUTS 'N BOLTS

Good communicators, like skilled artisans, utilize specific techniques when performing their craft. For the actor, the definitions of *technique* most helpful to this discussion are:

1. The method of accomplishing a desired goal.

2. The execution of method or style in any art.

3. The manner in which technical details are treated.

There are hundreds of books that deal with the techniques involved in various acting methods. Building a Quality Core and understanding the Human Condition help the actor use those techniques by building a solid foundation of self to draw on. In this way, the use of technique, in whatever style or method, will not be without substance.

This is not to suggest that techniques are in any way inferior to the subjects we've tackled so far. They go hand in hand. The periodontist can know everything there is to know about the biology and physiology of the human mouth, but without instruments, X-rays, a nurse, and a spit-sink, it is hard to get the patient to sit still for gum surgery.

Patrick Swayze: Sometimes technique is crucial. Just think about it in love scenes. I found a long time ago that it doesn't matter if the actress or actor is a jerk, and it's hard to work with them because there's so much ego. All that matters is that the camera needs to read passion. That could be hatred, that could be disgust, that could be love, that could be enamored. That could be many, many things. All that matters is that the camera is reading that passion, that need and that desire. It doesn't have to be, "My god, I love this person." It can be, "My god, I can't stand this person." As long as there's fire. As long as there's something really happening.

In the beginning, it's about craft, it's about skill, it's about the simple techniques of and the craft of acting. And coming up with a performance. That's a thing you learn in acting class. You have to have the skill first. The same way that a clown diver, in order to have the ability to make the dive look funny, must be incredibly, technically proficient first.

And when you're first trying to get a career off the ground, when you're going into an office situation that is completely not conducive to coming up with any kind of performance, like cattle being run through, how are you going to find a way to feel good about yourself and that you deserve this role? When there are fifty other clones that are better looking than you are. The only way is this: know that while they've been looking in a mirror, you've been training your butt off. You've been busting it on every level you can to learn and gain a craft.

So, as Patrick would tell you, I would be remiss if I didn't at least mention the essential techniques actors should have at their disposal. The following rundown is by no means a complete exploration of the subject. It is, however, a compilation of the varied styles I have been involved with through the years and found valid as an actor, director, and teacher.

If you've heard some of these terms before, it is no small wonder. A study of their genealogy would lead you to discover that most are rooted in the teachings or writings of Constantin Stanislavski and Richard Boleslavsky. Their concepts were first introduced in this country by members of The Group Theatre and The Actor's Studio. Some of the more charismatic members of those two groups, such as Harold Clurman, Lee Strasberg, Stella Adler, Sandy Misner, and Uta Hagen, became disciples and teachers of what would later be termed "method acting." And from that core sprung myriad acting coaches, all retooling the original teachings into their own personal styles. In Los Angeles alone there must be twenty different established acting schools, along with hundreds of private coaches offering a plethora of "unique" classes teaching various approaches to scene study, improvisation, sense memory, monologues, on-camera techniques, commercial techniques, etc.

Like most actors in the late seventies and early eighties, I took many different classes, studied many different books and learned from a variety of different teachers. I would have to say that my strongest influences were Florence M. Sikes (my first acting coach), The Actor's Studio, The Beverly Hills Playhouse, and the teachings/writings of Lee Strasberg, Uta Hagen, Stella Adler, Robert Lewis, and, of course, Stanislavski. Although I would be at a loss to immediately pinpoint the origin of many of the acting terms below, suffice it to say that I am very grateful to these individuals and schools in passing along the knowledge and spirit that certainly originated with Stanislavski and The Moscow Art Theatre.

TECHNIQUES RUNDOWN

Many successful, working actors have a "pilot's checklist" of techniques they feel must be accomplished for every new role. Lisa Rinna is one such actor. Lisa has appeared in nine films and numerous television shows. She is probably best known for her starring role as Taylor McBride on *Melrose Place*, and the two-time Soap Opera Digest Award-winning role of Billie Reed Brady on *Days of Our Lives*.

> *Lisa Rinna:* Acting class is like going to the gym. It's really important. During *Days of Our Lives*, I didn't have time to go to acting class. The soap opera was the acting class. I learned a huge amount just by having to go in there every day and confront everything that was given to me and just dive in and do it. I worked out every day for three years. When I got off the show, I did a movie then immediately studied Shakespeare for a month then got right back into acting class.
>
> When you learn, you get confidence from learning. And in turn you keep growing. That's what I want in my life. As long as I keep learning and growing in my work, I have the confidence to go out there and try new things.
>
> Through my study in various acting classes, I have a technique and an outline of how to come to a scene. How to break it down. I found that especially important when I was doing *Days of Our Lives* because you're just thrown into the show, so you gotta use your tools. That experience really taught me a lot.
>
> Basically, I have a number of questions that I ask myself about every scene. Specificity is everything in the work. And as long as I ask myself those questions, and I know where I'm coming from, then I have much less self-consciousness. I have a way of working that changes every time I work, but I have a base that I come from, always. A certain way that I emotionalize and prepare for certain emotional scenes. And I have to say that every time I work, even though I have this base that I come from, it's always different. I'm constantly learning.

Checklists are different for every actor, comprising different items and used at different points in the development process of each project. Some actors are very aware of their lists and mentally go about checking off each item as it is accomplished. Others have plied their craft for so long, the checklist is no longer a conscious effort. The techniques for these actors become second nature and a natural part of their creations.

In any case, these are some of the most commonly used techniques today. They are in no particular order of importance.

THREE-READ RULE

Patrick Swayze: I go at it very analytically. I approach the movie and every other character and relationship before I ever even look at my character. I try to allow the movie and what's demanded and required of the story to tell me who I need to be. And then I'm in tune with the overall vision, as opposed to just going with my own little vision that's just about protecting my own little performance. That's a process I've come to over years. I used to have to eat the furniture to try and get to the right place in the scene. And now I realize that that right place is always there. You just have to take the barriers away.

Too often, the inexperienced actor will read a script for the first time with little or no regard for story development, the other characters, the project's overall sensibilities, etc. Instead, all focus will be trained on the one role that actor is considering. Many actors actually highlight their parts during an initial read. Their big concern actually seems to be the number of lines their character utters and the monologues they will have a chance to emote.

The highly trained actor will read a script *at least three times* before thinking about performance.

The first read gives an overall sense of the piece. Is the story interesting? Is the writing well crafted? Do I like the message? As a whole, is this a project I would like to be involved in?

The second read gives a better sense of the relationships involved. What relationship do the characters have with themselves and each other? What are all the different relationship through-lines and how do they relate to one another?

The third read focuses on the integrity and disposition of the reader's particular role. Special attention is paid to the character's actions and idiosyncrasies, what the character says about herself/himself, and what other characters in the story say about that character. Here the actor begins to delve into the particular wants and needs of the character.

Subsequent reads may deal with historical aspects, regional concerns such as clothing and accents, stylistic concerns with the story's era, type of presentation, such as comedy, drama, mystery, musical, etc.

The point here is that it requires many reads to become fully invested—before the actor begins to worry about winning an Oscar or Tony. Question upon question must be asked and answered, both before accepting the role and throughout the rehearsal process.

STYLE

A mode of expression. The distinctive or characteristic mode of presentation, construction or execution in any art.

The type of project shades every element within its make-up. Actors who have a broad base of knowledge in theatre history as well as the history of cinema and the arts find it much easier to adjust their craft to the particular style of the piece.

For instance, all comedies are not equal. There are "light" comedies, "dark" comedies, "black" comedies, "high" comedies, comedy of errors, comedy of manners, genteel comedies, slapstick comedies, comedy dramas, burlesque, and "French chase" comedies. There are distinctions between Old, Middle, and New Comedy. There are fascinating differences between Greek, Roman, Renaissance, Commedia dell'Arte, Elizabethan, and Restoration comedies. And comedy is only one type of presentation. There are just as many distinctions in drama, mystery, science fiction, horror, action-adventure, romance, etc.

Each particular style dictates a different approach to the work. And it is very possible that a project includes more than one style. In any case, very specific choices must be made by the actor to incorporate his character and craft into different styles in terms of attitude, relationships, points of view, behavior, and so on.

ENVIRONMENT

Every scene takes place in a specific location with unique attributes that surround and influence the characters, dialogue, and action.

An intimate knowledge of the environment engenders confidence and natural behavior. It also frees the actor from technical concerns, allowing for more exciting choices in the work.

Actors use many techniques to become more familiar with a scene's environment. One of the most effective is to spend time, outside of the project, actually living the life of the character. For example, if the actor is cast as a short-order cook, time will be taken before rehearsals begin to work for a few hours or a few days as a cook in a local diner. The experiences, muscle memories, sense memories and affective memories of the sights, sounds, smells, manipulation of utensils, heat of the grill, etc., can then be transferred to the character, the set, and the project.

When the actor doesn't have the time or ability to live the character outside the project, a simpler exercise requires spending time alone on the set, away from rehearsals and performance, improvising a moment or an activity. In this way the actor comes to have a stronger connection with the set's surroundings and its props.

IMPROVISATION

The art of acting out a scene or circumstance
without a script or formalized outline.

The ability to improvise is a marvelous tool. Highly trained actors and directors use improvisation to explore and discover new and exciting possibilities inherent in specific characters or entire scenes.

RELAXATION

The physical body is the only "via" an actor has to express core qualities. Relaxation techniques are used when the actor's ability to perform is hampered by tensions that restrict the flow of emotions or communication.

The Olympic runner stretches before every race to loosen the muscles, allowing the body to perform at maximum capacity. The singer vocalizes the scales to warm up the voice before every singing engagement. So must the actor loosen the muscles of body and voice, as well as clear the mind of anxieties so that the instrument is free to communicate the actor's will.

All good actors have their own personal methods of relaxation. Some physically stretch, others use breathing exercises, some meditate, and still others use a combination of the three. There are hundreds of avenues for actors to discover relaxation techniques that work best for them: books, classes, personal trainers, gurus and so on. *How* an actor prepares the body and mind is personal. *That* the actor prepares the body and mind is essential.

OBJECTIVES

The actor must find actionable goals for the character to obtain in every scene. These goals or objectives should involve the simple task of living "in the moment" as well as hidden agendas the character strives to achieve in the story's relationships. For example:

There is a wonderful scene in the film *Victor/Victoria* when James Garner and Julie Andrews meet for the first time at an opening night reception. She has just finished a performance masquerading as a man and must continue the ruse as long as she is in public. Garner has just witnessed the performance and, dubious that Andrews is really a man because he felt a sexual attraction to her, decides he must meet her up close and personal.

The obvious surface objectives for both actors center around enjoying the reception: milling about, drinking champagne, making idle chitchat with strangers and each other.

The hidden agenda objectives for Garner focus on his need to find out if Andrews is really a woman, by such covert actions as squeezing her hand too tightly during a handshake, and asking tricky questions. Andrews' hidden agenda objectives revolve around the necessity to make everyone believe she is really a man, by her mannerisms, vocal quality, dress, etc.

THE STANISLAVSKI THREE

The whole key of playing surprise is the same key as playing drunk. That is, you don't play drunk. Any drunk is trying to look sober. So that takes you back to Elia Kazan's concept of, "You're character is revealed by how you conceal the emotion." We as human beings don't wear our emotions on our sleeves.

Patrick Swayze: So what I try to do up front is define all my problems or concerns with the scene. And not say, "I'm right." Just define all the problems so that the director's eye can look from his point of view and my point of view and help me come up with the right blend, the right feel. That's where all the design comes in. Storyboarding your emotional life, in a way. Yet, when the camera rolls you've got to have the courage to throw that away. Otherwise you run a huge risk of the performance being by rote. Or not being organic. Or not having that unpredictable dangerous quality which every actor needs. What makes an actor exciting to watch is when you never know what they're going to do next.

Lisa Rinna: What makes an actor fascinating is having an emotional life going on that he's in touch with. There's something going on that he's connected to, in his gut, emotionally, that is available and open and stirs something inside. An acting coach of mine once said, "It's like someone's on stage playing a violin, and you're sitting out in the audience. When they pluck those strings, you can feel it in your body. Your body actually picks up the vibration of that violin." And that's what good acting is all about. You're up there conveying, or you're playing your violin and the audience is getting the vibration of it.

I also think actors that are fascinating have an interesting physical life going on, which I'm really just starting to get into in my work. It's interesting to make choices physically. It's so subtle at times. Fascinating actors are always doing something, because in life people are always doing something. When you specifically physicalize the character, it brings that character to life. Those two things: emotionality and physicality.

Stanislavski suggested the actor answer three questions about every character's existence:

1. *What is the character's inner life?* What is the character feeling inside? To answer this question, the actor must explore such elements as the character's quality core, history, relationships, and feelings about current story dynamics.

2. *What is the character's outer life?* The outer life is a direct physical manifestation of the character's inner life. Mannerisms, speech pattern, hairstyle, dress, attitudes, actions and reactions are some of the outer life elements affected by a character's inner life.

3. *What is the character's physical life?* In what physical condition is the character? Is the character exhausted, exhilarated, beaten, drugged, in pain, etc.? And what are the physical manifestations of the character's state?

THE PREVIOUS MOMENT(S)

What happened to the character just before the scene? Often, the previous moment will dictate how a character enters a room and reacts to the situation. Sometimes a previous moment will affect an entire scene. For example, in a scene from the film *A Few Good Men*, Tom Cruise comes home late to find his partners have been patiently waiting for him to continue trial preparations. The "previous moment" for Tom's character includes aimlessly walking around in a downpour while drinking a fifth of bourbon after learning that his star witness has committed suicide. So during the scene, Tom's character is angry, soaked to the bone, and quite inebriated.

BEHAVIOR

What are all the physical actions the character is involved with during the scene? What tasks does the character perform to move the scene along or keep the scene from progressing? What activities involve the character while the scene unfolds?

One of the black-belt masters of behavior was Marlon Brando. Watch many of his films and you will see characters rich in physical performance. In *The Godfather*, the old dOon cuts up an orange to use as "monster teeth" while playing with his grandson. *On the Waterfront* finds him toying with Eva Marie Saint's glove as they have an intimate conversation while sitting on playground swings.

TEXT

Quite simply, what is the scene about? What is the apparent overall event and individual character events that make up the surface of the scene? Is it a funeral? Is it a party? What is the apparent reason for the character's presence?

In *The Godfather*, Al Pacino has dinner in a small Italian restaurant with a corrupt cop and a member of another Mafia family. The apparent overall event is eating a nice, quiet meal. Pacino's individual character event is to forge a truce between his family and these two gentlemen. Therefore, he speaks in gentle tones and, when he needs to use the bathroom, asks to go in a humble manner.

Once the questions of text are answered, acting choices can be made in terms of dress, behavior, attitude, relationships, etc.

SUBTEXT

The subtext of the scene is made up of the character's hidden agenda. What is the scene really about for the character? Why is the character really there? Are there counter intentions? Underlying truths? Covert actions that only the character and audience know about?

Getting back to that restaurant scene in *The Godfather*, Pacino is not really interested in having a nice meal and discussing a truce. The real reason he is there is to murder the two men he is dining with. He is only pleasant not to arouse suspicion. He politely asks to be excused because the gun he must use is hidden in the bathroom.

Subtext creates the dynamics inherent in drama and comedy. Subtext shows a level of emotions and behavior apparent only to the audience. The best actors find detailed text and subtext in every scene.

CEILING VALUES

Every choice the actor makes must be accompanied by the question, "How much?" or "How pressing?" The technique is called "ceiling values" because the choice made should be of the highest level possible, just short of "over the top" for that particular character.

How Much? In Neil Simon's comedy, *The Odd Couple*, the humor is sparked by and directly proportional to the differences between the personalities of the messy Oscar Madison and the finicky Felix Unger.

How much does Oscar hate Felix's cleanliness and melancholy? How much does he love sports, being a slob, and playing poker? Each decision should then manifest itself in the actor's choices regarding attitudes and behavior.

Example: Felix's fetish for cleanliness drives Oscar to the point of wiping his shoes on the curtains, spitting on a framed picture, and throwing a plate of spaghetti against the wall.

How Pressing? The issue of urgency must also be addressed in every scene. A sense that the character's objectives must be accomplished immediately or suffer dire consequences, adds a wonderful dynamic to the work.

Example: In John Grisham's film, *The Pelican Brief*, in which Julia Roberts plays a law student whose brief (her theory about the conspiracy behind an assassination of two Supreme Court Justices) puts her life in jeopardy. Much of the story is a race against time; pitting her search for the truth against the forces that are trying to murder her. The knowledge of imminent danger creates a pressing desire to accomplish her objectives and creates a high sense of awareness and drama.

THE AUDITION

Unnatural! That's the best way I've heard it described. Oh, I've heard other words like *nerve-racking, humiliating, inane,* and even *violating*. But *unnatural* makes the most sense.

Think about it. What other profession requires a complete show of one's abilities, on the spot, before being hired? Does the hospital administrator require the prospective doctor to extract someone's spleen during the interview while lightheartedly discussing his attributes? Does the contractor demand that the prospective builder quickly construct a house just to show what the work would be like if hired to erect the real building? And through it all, knowing that even if the splenectomy goes without a hitch, even if the structure built is beautiful and will last a thousand years, the job may go to someone else because they are...*taller!* Or prettier or uglier or fatter or skinnier or sexier or too sexy.

That's not going to happen, right? That would be cruel and inhumane, *right?* Well, to the performer, it's par for the course. The performer isn't allowed to show up with only his resume in hand and a pleasant disposition. No, no, no. The performer must perform. And be gracious about the whole nerve-racking, humiliating, unnatural process. And be *perfect*. Is it any wonder performers spend most of their waking hours stressing and obsessing about their next audition?

There is a plethora of how-to books on the subject of auditions, delving into specific techniques designed to help the performer give the best "splenectomy" possible under the most stressful conditions. Mastering technique in any profession is vital, and I would highly recommend honing those skills specific to the audition process.

Equally important is gaining a realistic understanding of how the casting director views the audition process. I have always suggested to my clients that if they want to be more comfortable with auditions, they should spend a bit of time on the other side of the fence. Work for a casting director. Sit in on as many auditions as possible. Listen to what is said about the performers after they're gone. What you hear will amaze you.

As co-owner of one of the busiest casting companies in Los Angeles, Ann Wilkinson has spent the past eleven years finding talent for commercials, television shows, and films. Her company, Tepper-Gallegos Casting, handles approximately 125 individual casting jobs each year. Although they specialize in casting commercials for products such as Welch's Grape Juice, McDonald's, Honda, Huggies, and Hallmark Cards, Tepper-Gallegos has completed projects for NBC, Paramount, Tri-Star, Columbia, CBS, and Universal Studios. Miss Wilkinson's experience and expertise afford a unique perspective on the sensibilities of the casting director and the dynamics of the audition process:

Ann Wilkinson: What I see in an audition that makes an actor interesting enough to cast, and in the people that I see booked and then see working as actors, is a basic confidence that is very strong. Confidence in an audition is, not needing the job. It's the ability to adapt very quickly to the given situation and to maintain one's own personality. Many times actors will come in, and they are so willing to please that they will let go of their personality in an attempt to be whatever it is that will get them the job. You will see that ninety-nine times out of a hundred. They may be good actors and do exactly what is written, but they're not giving it any life. It just remains flat because it doesn't have the added dimension that makes it a little different. They are doing action and dialog, and it's perfect, but there's no surprise to it.

Now, the people who walk through the door and manage to maintain a sense of themselves within the audition,...yes, they'll do what the director asks them to do but they'll do it with their own little twist. It's the confidence. Just comes right back to feeling like they are in the right place doing the right thing. And, that they were the right person to be picked. Those are the people who can maintain their personal confidence. Every set I've ever been on, everything is falling apart all the time. There is always this slight note of desperation and yes, they do try to separate that from the actor most of the time. But it starts to creep around. If the actor can just maintain, and not get hooked into it or upset by it. It's the confidence of, "I'm here, I'm doing a good job, people are interested in watching me." The sense that they have a right to be the center of attention for those two or three minutes of time. A sense that they are worthy of it, and entertaining. Those are the people who are immediately interesting to watch. Everything they do is a little quirky. It's a little different. What they do is complete because they're bringing themselves to it.

It has to be confidence in a way that is not arrogant. There is a fine line there because there is an energy level from that confidence that will fill up the room. But if it goes just a little too far, it will have an opposite effect. Then their reputation precedes them. What will happen is you'll have an actor who may not be really good, but is a really nice person, and is consistently on time, and consistently tries really hard, and you end up trying hard for them. "Oh, he's such a nice guy, I hope he gets a job." "Let's bring him in, one of these days it will work for him!"

Whereas the people who come in, and maybe that confidence takes them across the line and they're a little difficult because of it, they start to get an attitude like, "I just got here, but I've got to leave," or "I'm only here for twenty minutes so don't waste my time." This is a small business and that attitude gets around.

There is an actress who used to work a lot. When I started casting she was the commercial queen. You know—if you were doing a spot for a mom or for a spokeswoman in her thirties, you had her in for the audition. Well, she was just incredibly difficult. And what happened was, as soon as the worm turned, and it always does, she had been so difficult for all those years that people weren't willing to go those extra two or three steps for her, to help her break her slump.

So, being difficult has to do with attitude; it's being grumpy in the waiting room. It's fussing about the fact that they've had to wait for a few minutes. It's not getting there on time. It's sitting out there and gossiping with their friends and not looking over their script, then walking through it instead of really knowing it. It's not being prepared. And it's the attitude that, "My way is better." Instead of it being probably what all of us are really looking for, which is a combined effort. The casting director offers ideas and then the actor takes and incorporates those ideas and brings them to life and adds those special little twists that are a surprise and make it interesting for you as well. A person is difficult if their ideas are the only ideas.

And what gives the performer that feeling of confidence so coveted by the casting director?

Ann Wilkinson: Practice. It just comes with practice. Whether it's taking classes or doing showcases or, if you are interested in being a speaker, joining Toastmasters. You have to practice. You have to hone your craft. I do find that the people who are willing to hone their craft are the ones who end up working. It should be something you really like doing, and it's fun for you to do, whether or not you ever make a penny from it. You should be able to walk in confidently, and know what you're suppose to do before you walk into the room. Practice, practice, practice. That will give you the confidence.

Once a performer gets a thumbs-up from the casting director the part is secured and life is grand, right? *Wrong.* Most accomplished performers will tell you that casting directors are usually just the first stepping stone to getting a major role. What of directors, producers, and writers? They all want their say. And they usually get it. In fact, the number of auditions the performer must endure is usually proportional to the size of the role or the magnitude of the project. And with so many chefs in the kitchen, it's a wonder anything actually gets made. So the actor must endure several more auditions to appease those involved in the actual making and funding of the project.

So what of those second and third auditions? What is wanted and needed from the actor? I've already introduced you to Allan Katz, Vahan Moosekian and Ronnie Clemmer, all accomplished writers, directors, and producers, and all very opinionated on the subject of these auditions. If you'll remember, Allan is our resident expert on the situation comedy audition, having produced/written shows such as *M*A*S*H*, The Fresh Prince of Bel Air, Blossom,* and *Roseanne*:

> *Allan Katz*: The hope is that sometimes it's just the person. They just come in and they own it. So that it ends up being different and better than what it was on paper.
>
> It's very rare to find an actor who hasn't done comedy and who isn't funny in real life...funny, charming or whatever, who can come in and do a comedy. It's like somebody who was never an athlete starring in *The Natural*. You know he won't be able to throw the ball the right way, won't be able to pitch, won't be able to hit. He doesn't have the physique for it, he doesn't have the focus for it. He's not an athlete! There are some people who are not comics. There are some dramatic actors or personalities who are really charming, but as soon as you put them in a comedy they become absolutely dreadful! It's just unfamiliar territory; something they haven't done or they haven't had a need to do.
>
> That's why it's so hard to find a leading man who can also do comedy. You can name them on one hand because usually, when you're good looking, you don't have to reach for that stuff for attention. If you're a Tom Cruise there is no reason to develop a different persona. You've got yourself a great looking smile, you look terrific and the girls like you. You're bright and charming so you don't have to be funny. You don't have to wait for the laugh. You don't have to push it a bit. As a consequence, you don't have much life experience making people laugh.

When you look at standups, for the most part they are pretty eccentric looking people. Not eccentric like a Marty Feldman, but eccentric in the sense that they are unusual. They are the class clown, they use intelligence, they use something or other to get people to notice or recognize them. So it's not by accident that so many irregular-looking people, including myself, have gone into comedy. We've had to find a different tact so that we will be interesting.

Now, when you get the combination of somebody who is attractive in a more classic sense, not that everybody has to be Tom Cruise gorgeous, but when somebody like that can do comedy, it's incredible. That's why there are some people, like a Tom Hanks, who time after time after time hit a home run. And even when they don't, you still want to go see them do it because you say, "I love it! I really love this guy!"

I do have a couple of pet peeves when it comes to the audition process. Some of them bother me because I don't think they give actors the best shot at doing the job. Which means it doesn't give me the best shot at knowing what they have.

It is always better when you come in for an audition that you know the material. It breaks moments of acting when you are still on book. You are still looking at pages and you get lost. Sometimes you don't have the choices. You come in and you are rushing around and you get the sides last minute. The best service you can do for yourself if you haven't had enough time to prepare is to find out if you can have more time. I don't think that it serves you well to say that you will do it anyway. You have to do everything you can to give yourself the best shot. That means if you can take the time, if you can reschedule, if somebody else that is prepared can go in before you do, you should sit there and spend a little bit more time with the material. It is foolish not to.

The other thing that happens is, if you prematurely try to get off the page and try to dance around it, and you screw up the words and you screw up the language; you sometimes lose the joke or you lose the scene or you lose whatever is going on. And then it isn't funny. I have no way of knowing whether you can do it or not. For all I know, you are one of those kinds of actors that show up and the script isn't a script. The script is just something to screw around with until you get what you want. I have no idea whether you have respect for material, whether you can make it work, or whether you can add something to the material that helps.

Now it doesn't bother me if somebody puts a couple of words in or changes something around. As long as it doesn't feel to me like a criticism of the material, as much as it is a way of putting a little bit of a spin on it or getting it to sound a little bit more like what your character can do with it. You have to be careful because sometimes that material is crafted so that the joke is at the very end of the sentence. Sometimes you think it is kind of funny to say it in your own way so that the joke ends up being in the middle of the sentence. When you get through, you have a lot of words hanging out there and nobody can laugh. If you don't understand comedy, you kill yourself! You do yourself a real disservice. What I am saying is that if you don't understand it, don't screw with it! And if you do understand it, don't screw with it.

It is always good to ask, "Is there anything you want to tell me?" Because sometimes in the process, from the time the material has gone out till now, we may have seen a number of different ways. That way you know that there is some flexibility. There is some kind of range. Rather than just walking in and taking a shot at it. Unless you are really prepared. I sometimes feel, when people come in and they sort of breeze in and breeze out, that they don't want to be there. Now, I don't mean schmoozing. They don't have to do that. If someone comes in and says, "Okay, I'm ready," I figure maybe that is their style. Maybe they've peaked and want to go on and do it. But sometimes they miss getting the information. They miss settling down a little bit. I guess that is more for the individual to decide.

Also, I don't expect people to wear suits. I don't expect that they be freshly pressed. But there is this grunge style of wearing clothes for an audition that really puts me off. The clothes look like they haven't been washed in weeks and the actor comes in with a couple of days worth of facial hair growth.

Now, this may be their "lucky audition outfit," but unless that is the character, it puts me off in the same way it would if I were sitting next to somebody like that in a restaurant. It is really hard to warm up to somebody like that, especially when I'm doing comedy. I've got to sit there and look at somebody and think, "What will this guy look like if he was cleaned up?" "Is this the way he normally is?" and "Is this somebody the audience is going to respond to? Because I'm uncomfortable around him!"

I have seen people come in T-shirts with holes in them that were dirty, and hair that was filthy. It just shows lack of respect, unless you are living in your car. If you are living in your car you still should be able to get a razor. I have had people come in who have done a really good job at reading, and I've called the agent and said, "I would like to see this actor again, and have him clean himself up!" I'm shocked by it. It is a lack of respect for themselves, the material and the whole profession. I just look at that and it affects how I look at the character. It makes me wonder if this is what this actor thinks this character is. It all fits together. All that kind of stuff says so much about who you are, how you approach the material, and what your range is.

So, for the situation comedy audition, Allan suggests the actor know the material, if at all possible do the material as written, and come to the reading well-groomed. Seems simple enough. And what about auditions for the prime-time drama? Vahan Moosekian has produced myriad television series since 1984:

Vahan Moosekian: I think if the essence is there, it's there. You have people who go to great lengths when they come in to audition. When people come in to read for a lead they tend to just dress somewhat appropriately. If they come in for just a small part they will bring in props and costumes. It is funny. If you've got the look then you've got the look. If you don't, you don't. It is just that simple. When casting, you look for the essence.

By the way, sometimes it goes the other way too. I can ask the casting director to give me a guy to play a judge. All the old guys come in wearing glasses and have gray around the temples and then, just for the hell of it, what we end up saying is we want to make it an African-American woman. You know that woman who read for the doctor, I don't think she is right for that part but why don't we try her as the judge? So, sometimes we go in a crazy direction or go off beat. Sometimes a guy will come in and he will look completely different than what we had in mind but we just go, "Why don't we go that way with it and make it more interesting?"

In general, if you are going for a lawyer, I would go in a coat and a tie. Don't come in jeans and a T-shirt. It goes against it. You could come in a sport coat without a tie. In film the camera is too close to you to put on airs. You can't project it. You can't act it. You just have to be that person or close enough to that person.

This is something an actor should really understand. I always tell actors not to blow themselves out of the water because they didn't get a part. There is so much to choose from. It may be that the color of your eyes was the reason you didn't get it. Maybe you were a little taller than the guy we were going to cast so it was your height and there is nothing you can do about that. If I'm casting a part for a leading role I'm looking for the actor who is the most interesting, has the most colors, is going to surprise me a little bit, is going to bring something fresh, a different interpretation that we didn't think of, to the role.

If I'm casting a role that will have two or three lines and is supposed to be a doctor, I'm going to cast somebody who I believe looks like a doctor, because that character doesn't have the character development that is going to tell anything about him. We're going to put him in a white coat and a stethoscope because we are just trying to sell the idea right away that the other character is talking to a doctor. Sometimes based on that I will cast something just on looks. If I bring in a female brain surgeon and I cast Cindy Crawford, who doesn't sound like a doctor, doesn't look like a doctor, doesn't look like she belongs in a white smock, I'm doing myself a disservice. If I cast somebody who looks the part and can convince the audience instantly that she is a doctor, then that is who I am going to cast. It just sells the audience right away.

My advice to people who audition for me? Be yourself and bring what you can to the role. Bring confidence to the performance. I like actors, particularly in television, who are theatrically trained. With movies you can do fifty takes and you can experiment with it, so it's possible to hire somebody who has never acted before and get away with it. On television we don't have time. We will shoot seven pages a day and shoot an entire show in seven days. The actor has got to get it immediately. And to do that, he must have a certain craft about him.

Mr. Moosekian wants the actors who audition for him to be trained, be themselves and not obsess if they don't get the part. Easier said than done, but doable nonetheless. And what of feature films? Ronnie Clemmer's producing credits include *A Child's Cry for Help*, *An Unfinished Affair*, and *A League of Their Own*.

Ronnie Clemmer: You walk in nervous, trying to win the job. For you this may be life or death. You may have that mortgage payment due next week, and if you don't get this job you don't know how you are going to pay it. You may have had five rejections in a row, and if you don't get this job you're going back to Dubuque. All of those things are irrelevant to me as a producer. Not because I don't care but because that is not my life. My job is not to help you pay your mortgage. My job is to find the best actor so that I can have the best scene so my movie will do the best. And I can stay alive as a company and have more auditions for more actors to get jobs.

When you come in, you want to divorce yourself from the personal emotions that you bring to an interview situation or an audition situation and focus on the job. It helps me, too. It relieves me of the anxiety of watching you under anxiety, and I can evaluate your craft and your performance and not worry about you as a human being, which rarely helps you. It often makes me worry if this person is going to be able to focus on the set. Is this person going to be able to perform in spite of the mortgage payment that is due?

The person coming into the room has to also understand that it is a lot less personal than you would think. The thing that a person should do is to relax, be comfortable, be focused, figure out what I need and do the performance. It is an audition. It is not brain surgery. When you come in you may have done a great job. When you leave the room the producer may say, "He did a great job. But our female star is three inches taller than he is and that's not going to work. This is not "Blue Lagoon" where we can cut trenches in the sand for Brooke Shields so she is not taller than the male star."

The choices I make may have to do with the fact that you are good, but we are thinking about getting that raven-haired female and I want a salt and pepper contrast. If we decide to go with the blonde then you are number one or two on my list. If we go with the brunette, you move to five or six on my list. You may leave the room and say, "I thought I did great. I nailed that performance!" Then you don't hear anything. And three days later I'm still trying to decide, "Do I get that blonde or the brunette?" Until I set that deal, I can't decide on the guy. Four days later you are sitting at home saying to yourself, "What is the matter with those guys? I know I nailed it. What do these people know? I'm getting out of the business!" You are kicking your own butt, and it has nothing to do with your talent.

Knowing that you can't control the multiple factors that are on my side of the desk gives you permission to do your best and walk away hands clean. There is nothing for you in figuring out how I made my choices. It is what makes the life of an actor so difficult. If you are going to be an actor, accept the parameters of the job. You are not in control. All you can do is be in control of your life, your performance, your focus and your emotions. You can't control anything else, so why waste the energy? You will never know why, and you will kill yourself psychologically and physiologically and make yourself less prepared for the next audition. Do your best, focus, walk away, and let it go.

Of all the audition advice given so far, Ronnie Clemmer's should probably be at the top of the list. "Do your best, focus, walk away, and let it go." This isn't to diminish the use of technique and craft. In fact, Mr. Clemmer believes them to be essential:

Many times actors think, "I'm not as pretty as she is," or "I'm not as handsome as he is." The greatest actors are not always the prettiest or most handsome people. They are the most commanding. They are the most engaging. Some of that is genetic. There is something about their face on camera that makes you want to watch more of them. Genetically you can't change that, but the performance can also be a factor. I don't think Steve Buscemi would be called by anyone a handsome performer, but he has a way of assuming a person that is so engaging. That is what he brings to it. His craft, not only his art, but his craft brings it to the table.

Ronnie Clemmer: Those communicators who stayed much saner in the fields of both media and acting have done so because they approached it as a craft. A craft to be learned, a craft to be improved, a craft to be practiced at all times, not just waiting for the big movie, and a craft to be perfected. In Hollywood we tend to emphasize the stardom and the glamour that surrounds the performance. It is about what you get to do before the performance and what gets written about afterwards. The press coverage, the *People Magazine* article, the Barbara Walters interview becomes as important in this country as the actual performance on screen. Therefore the stardom starts taking over in place of the craft, the work. When people start getting distracted by that, they can lose focus on the craft. The performance suffers and their self-confidence suffers because they are now playing the game of being a star instead of working on the craft of acting. That is the first part of it. The second part of it is the art. There is a lot of art in these things but it is the craft that gets you to the art. Michelangelo didn't sit around and practice being a gifted artist. He sat around practicing hands. He practiced eyes. He practiced faces. And it was that attention to detail and focus and work on the craft, combined with his natural innate gift, which gave us the Sistine Chapel.

Quality Keys

Fervency of the journey is the goal when on the road to mastery.

- *Techniques* go hand in hand with the *communicator's* quality core and Human Condition, building a solid foundation of "self" to draw on for any craft.

- *3-read rule* Read a script *at least three times* before thinking about performance.

- *Style* A mode of expression. The distinctive or characteristic mode of presentation, construction or execution in any art.

- *Environment* Every scene takes place in a specific location with unique attributes that surround and influence the characters, dialogue and action.

- *Improvisation* Acting out a scene or circumstance without script or outline.

- *Relaxation* Relaxation techniques are used when the actor's ability to perform is hampered by tensions or constrictions that restrict the flow of emotion and communication.

- *Objectives* Actionable goals for the character to attempt in every scene. Simple tasks of living "in the moment" as well as the character's hidden agendas.

- *Inner life* What the character is feeling inside.

- *Outer life* A direct physical manifestation of the character's inner life.

- *Physical life* The physical condition of the character. Also, the physical manifestations of the character's state.

- *Previous moment* What happened before the scene, affecting the character's present time behavior.

- *Behavior* The character's physical actions.

- *Text* The apparent overall event and individual character events that make up the surface of the scene.

- *Subtext* A character's hidden agenda.

- *Ceiling Values* An actor's choice should be accompanied by the question, "How much?" or "How pressing?"

THE AUDITION

- Constantly study: learn your craft and practice your art. Confidence is gained through this process.

- Be confident, not cocky.

- Rehearse, rehearse, rehearse. Know the material cold.

- Do the material as written.

- Arrive well groomed.

- Don't take it personally.

- Do your best, focus, walk away, and let it go.

8 THE ANCHOR

"WHO'S THE MOST DIFFICULT CLIENT FOR A TALENT COACH?" I'm asked that question at least once a month. And though I have worked with literally thousands of people over the years, there are only a handful whose names I wouldn't mind dragging through the mud. You'll find a list of those individuals in chapter—just kidding—maybe the next book.

At any rate, most clients/students fall into one of four categories: Entertainment (actors, show-hosts, personalities, etc.), Sports (athletes, coaches, etc.), Public Speakers (politicians, religious leaders, spokespeople, lecturers, etc.) or Television News (anchors, reporters, etc.). Profiling the characteristics of each, I would have to say that athletes are probably the easiest to get along with, for two reasons:

1. Communication is a whole new game to most athletes, and usually not within their realm of expertise. Therefore their egos are not as vulnerable, since we're not dealing with a subject they are all that familiar with.

2. If there is something athletes understand better than anyone else on this planet, it is the value of a coach and the process of

practice. Most of their lives revolve around those two concepts. Great athletes know how to put their respect and trust into that one person who will lead/motivate them to success. Great athletes know how to listen, absorb, utilize and do.

Many sports fans were recently surprised to learn that Troy Aikman (three-time Super Bowl winner) recently took on a specialized athletic coach just to hone basic skills. It is unfortunate that so few in our country have the same high regard for continuing education and self-improvement as Aikman. The very nature of a master, in any field, revolves around the thirst for knowledge, the joy of learning, and the need for constant nurturing of one's spirit and craft. Go Troy!

Public speakers are also fairly easy to coach. Their very existence revolves around communicating a message they truly believe. When they are grounded in that message, it can translate into a powerful fervency that is very compelling. Presentation problems will sometimes occur when they have to deliver a message that is not as close to their hearts, taking them away from their own core. Because they have a deep need for approval and a willingness to do whatever it takes to be believed, when coaching is sought after it is greatly appreciated.

The level of coaching difficulty soars as we move on to actors. Reason being, everything is subjective and intimate to the actor. This is understandable since most actors tend to work from the inside out, grounding their craft with personal experience. Difficulty, by the way, does not mean drudgery. The entertainment field is most exciting for the coach because the students/clients are so diversified in their personalities, needs, and goals. And because there's really no one style or method suitable for every individual, of the four groups, working with entertainers calls on the coach to be the most creative.

And then there are anchors...

TAIL WAGGING THE CAT

Cat owners know the scene all too well: Their little fur-ball stalks a bird in the front yard. Crouching low while slowly creeping toward the possibility of a mid-afternoon snack, the cat's tail suddenly shoots straight up and swishes back and fourth in the air, startling the bird. The cat is then dumbfounded and frustrated when its frightened prey flies away.

Feline psychologists (yes, they do exist) tell us that uncontrollable tail wagging in cats signifies acute conflict. Cats by their very nature are close-quarter pouncers. They like to wait in high brush for their prey to come to them. The internal conflict for urban kitties arises when their uncontrollable urge to hunt must be satisfied on manicured lawns. Without natural cover, the cat is forced into the unnatural behavior of crawling toward its prey in the open. Halfway to Nirvana, Fluffy overloads and "the tail wags the cat."

Anchors who have actually gone through the rigors of journalistic education and experience are trained to make sure the information they disseminate is pure and unbiased. Viewers, on the other hand, want more than just data. They want more than just a good reader giving them those data. They want someone with a heart for what he is reporting. Viewers not only want the story, they want a great storyteller. In fact, the *Parade Magazine* reported that 82 percent of the television-viewing public think reporters are insensitive to people's pain when covering disasters and accidents.[13] Bill Taylor, chairman of the board of Media Advisors International,[14] reports that twenty years of research points to the same thing: People want their news coverage from anchors who understand, are interested in, and care about the stories they tell.

Talk about internal conflict! On the one hand, the "journalist's code" (unwritten but understood) mandates that anchors be unbiased. On the other hand, viewers demand anchors have empathy. If anchors had cat's tails, they'd beat themselves silly.

Ronnie Clemmer: When I was a reporter, people watching the six o'clock news did not care how bad a night I had the night before. They didn't care if I had a difficult day trying to get all the videotape gathered. They didn't care if my cameraman got sick half way through the shoot. That was not their concern. All they cared about was, "Give me a concise, coherent newscast. Tell me what I need to know!" In fact, that was the job; to eliminate for the viewer all the distractions. Focus on what it is you are communicating and give them information.

Now, there is an art that goes with the craft. Once we have set the disciplined framework of what we are trying to achieve, once we have set the parameters, that is the disciplined part. That is your craft. Then what you get in that moment, sometimes following up a question, is far more important than the question that was conceived to begin with. Sometimes knowing how to listen is far more important than what you said. It is the ability to read off of someone to interact, not merely to act as a projection of ego. To be able to interact with another person is what separates the really high quality performer from the okay performer. Bring me the stuff I didn't know I wanted. And that's your art.

Anchors, as a group, are the most difficult to coach for this reason: it is perplexing for them to grasp the notion that *it is possible to be unbiased and convey the Human Condition* when telling a story. Their training and background give weight to the words they speak, but no one ever takes the time to explain what has just been explained to you in this book: the actual text of the script contributes to only 7 percent of the communication process.

Ronnie Clemmer: There are those who, like Chet Huntley or David Brinkley, bring to it an integrity of person. They bring intellect. That in and of itself is fascinating, intriguing, and convincing. Then there are some that you just enjoy hearing their point of view. There is a personality there. Oprah Winfrey is a very bright woman. We are not there just for her intellect but also for her performance. It is her personality. She is part of the act. She is not just the abstract newsperson or the channeler offering the news, she is part of the event.

There are two kinds of news people. Part of the problem with journalism today is figuring out how to differentiate. In the newspaper it is easy. There is the editorial page. And you know on that page you are hearing personality and a point of view. The rest of the paper is supposed to be clear, clean, intelligent and unbiased thinking. On television it is really difficult to draw those lines. The morning shows are becoming more and more where those lines are completely blurred. Is Bryant Gumbel the best objective interviewer of morning television, or the most assertively egocentric personality? It depends on your point of view.

The best blend of that is Katie Couric, who is smart, who started out in straight news, who has a great personality. People like listening to her talk about events and she can somehow make that magical transformation from, "Just getting the facts, Ma'am," to that brilliant personality who interacts with heads of state as well as heads of plumbing divisions. There are places where your personality, overlaid on the news, is totally inappropriate. I don't particularly want to know what Los Angeles anchor Paul Moyer was feeling when the bomb went off in Atlanta. That is getting in the way of my hearing what happened. Tell me as objectively as you can, as Dan Rather told us from the beaches of Galveston during the hurricane.

That basically made him a national newscaster after being a local newscaster in Houston. You can have some emotion, too, but tell me what's happening. Tell me, as Edward R. Murrow did from the bomb shelters of London, what's going on. I'll get what I need from the multiple and detailed descriptions. From the very literary descriptions he had, I could get the emotion of the report. Be an observer of detail. Even by the choosing of detail, we implant personality in our stories. It is what we observe that defines our perception. Give me the most details that you can and I will be able to make some conclusions. It is a hard line to walk, but I think it is an important one.

As I have stated before, I am not suggesting anchors accept poor writing or substandard journalistic skills. As far as I am concerned, those are critical elements that the anchor should possess for long-term success. This work assumes those skills are being mastered and need a strong voice. The Master Communicator has that voice. We have already determined Quality Core and the Human Condition are cornerstones the anchor, as communicator, must build on. This chapter offers specific concepts, tools, and techniques that anchors may utilize to further their progress on the road to mastery.

PORTRAIT OF AN ANCHOR

It never fails. And it usually comes just after the first critique and discussion of a recent newscast revealing many areas of opportunity for growth and development. The client will persevere in the recommendations for improvement, then ask for an example of a real-life anchor, in a local market, who actually embodies all the characteristics and elements that have been suggested. Sometimes the question arises because the client is dubious as to the existence of this "ideal" anchor. Other times the query is sincere. The client feels that observation of the "ideal" anchor in action will give a better understanding of the concepts and make them easier to integrate.

But none of that matters because I always refuse to give that kind of example in a first coaching session. There are two good reasons: 1. As we've discussed, what makes someone compelling and unique is the use of their own Quality Core, not someone else's. 2. The "ideal" anchor does not exist. The term suggests perfection, which negates the whole "Mastery is a Journey" concept. There is no Nirvana. Not on earth, anyway.

Now, I've worked with local anchors who are really wonderful: Sherri Allen at KTBS in Shreveport, Kendall Tenney at KVBC in Las Vegas, Bobbi Earls and Ron Steele at KWWL in Waterloo, Tim Irr and Sheila Grey at WSAZ in the Huntington/Charleston market, Guy Atchley and Colleen Bagnall at KGUN in Tucson—all are respected in their markets, respected in the newsroom, respected by their peers. But of all the anchors I've worked with on a local level, one of the closest to what I consider "ideal" is Don Shelby, WCCO's 6:00- and 10:00 P.M. anchor in Minneapolis.

Shelby has won all five of the nation's top journalism awards, including three National Emmys, The Columbia-DuPont Citation, the Scripps-Howard Award for Excellence, the George Foster Peabody Award,[15] and the Society of Professional Journalists Distinguished Service Award.[16]

In addition to his duties as WCCO-TV's weekday anchor, Shelby continues to report in the field. His reports on the orphans of Romania and the facially deformed children of Venezuela not only won accolades, but raised hundreds of thousands of dollars for the causes. As a result of the reports on the Romanian orphans, Minnesota families adopted more than 130 children.

Working with an organization called "Twin Cities 1 to 1," Shelby promotes the idea that mentored teens obtain better grades, raise their goals and are less likely to get into drugs. As a result, thousands of Minnesotans have volunteered to spend time with young people.

An avid outdoorsman, Shelby turned his interest in fishing into one of the largest and most prestigious bass tournaments in the country. The Don Shelby U.S. Invitational raised more than a half-million dollars for the Ronald McDonald House, so that families can stay with their children as they are treated for life-threatening illnesses.

There is more to Don's biography, but I think you get the idea. There is more to being an "ideal" anchor than delivering copy well during a newscast. Mastery must touch all aspects of the anchor's life, on and off the set.

THE COMMAND ANCHOR

The Command Anchor is a concept created by Audience Research & Development (AR&D), based on literally tens of thousands of interviews with viewers who commented on the qualities of "ideal" news anchors. The term "command" is derived from the viewer's perception that successful anchors are seen as "in command" of the material and substance in the newscast.

Don Shelby: I have a pretty good image of this market now. When I first started, my performance was generally based on what I thought was good professional conduct. I tried to have a pleasing voice. I tried to deliver in a crisp way for people to understand. I tried to not have an accent. I tried to hit the right words. I tried to sound like an announcer. I tried to make people feel comfortable that I was authoritative. I tried to do tricks and techniques to make them believe that was true of me. But 100 percent of my communication at that time was putting my act together and being a performer. Performing words. Performing lines. Acting.

As time went on and the longer I was able to live in a market, the more the market began to take on a sort of personality. And the more that you are out among the people who watch you, you get an idea of the things they hear and the things they don't hear. By their feedback, you know what they've missed and what they're seizing on. What they like and what they don't like. And after a period of time, you can develop sort of a personality profile. And develop, in essence, a listening profile for that audience. So, when I perform on the air now, I have a very clear image of the kind of person I'm speaking to.

The Command Anchor Concept takes all of the elements offered by the viewers as "ideal" and boils them down to the most common viewer "truisms." Therefore, viewers see the Command Anchor as the embodiment of three main facets:

The Gracious Host The anchor in this role is responsible for making viewers feel comfortable, so they can watch the news and absorb the information without distractions. Unlike the "ringmaster" concept, which relegates the anchor to simply introducing one story after another, here the anchor is a true host. The viewer sees the anchor as glad to be on-set doing this job, and obviously involved with the material. The anchor must keep the show moving smoothly, cover any gaffs that might occur, handle unforeseen circumstances, and make all who appear on-set or in the newscast feel welcome.

The Omniscient Observer The viewer perceives that the anchor sees and understands all that takes place during the newscast. In fact, as far as the viewer is concerned, the anchor has a big role in deciding which stories are to be covered and how they are presented. As the Omniscient Observer, the anchor is the "tie that binds" when it comes to history and context. The anchor understands why any story is important and why the viewer should be listening.

The Viewer's Representative In reviewing copy before the newscast, the anchor has a specific responsibility to raise the red flag if that copy is confusing or seems to assume knowledge. During the newscast, the anchor must listen and understand everything that happens. When questioning a reporter, the anchor must do so in a comfortable, layman-like manner, because at this point, the anchor is representing the viewer. The anchor asks questions to clarify those issues important to the viewer. The anchor is the champion of the viewer. The anchor's role is to make sure the flow of information is clear, understandable, and well delivered, with energy and commitment. All this must be done in a human, people-oriented style.

Don Shelby: If you are an average human being with the average sorts of foibles and failures and successes, the persona that is promoted on television and the stature that is given to that person in the anchor chair, and the trust that is given to that anchor, he should (and if he doesn't he'll fail) try to grow into that image. Try to make himself the person that people believe him to be.

By virtue of telephone calls and letters and personal meetings with people, they believe in me, for right or wrong. Or they believe in me because they see something substantially true that they like, or they believe in me because I'm the guy on television and they would have believed in anybody. Regardless of why they believe, they assume some things about you: They assume over a period of time, if you've managed to keep your nose clean, that you are a decent human being. That you are a fair and just human being; that you are a compassionate person; that you are a person of good moral standards. That you care for the people that you're working with; that you care for the community in which you live; that you love children. That you abide by the law; that you believe in the laws of the land. They begin to believe in you for lots of reasons. One, because that's the part that's promoted. That's the part that you're showing them. In real life there may be parts of you that don't fit that altogether.

So the object is to become as good as they think you are, because they really think you're terrific, and they really believe in you. And you want that after a period of time. If you live in the job and you're like me, you want that all to be true. You don't want to disappoint them. If you're a person on television you're a people-pleaser to start with. You're a person who wants acceptance and affection. And if they will like you more because you're honest and ethical, then you have a tendency to become more honest and ethical in your private life. And pretty soon you become who they want you to be.

It is the very simple "acting as if" program of behavioral modification. If you want to be a better person and you're not a good person now, simply act as if you are a better person and in no time you will in fact be that better person. By simply acting as if you are that better person. So I have spent, through the guidance of an audience, a long time acting as if I am the person they think I am. And I have become that person. I am now that person.

THE ANCHOR GROWTH MODEL

The anchor must master specific fundamentals in order to become dominant in the viewer's mind and in the viewer's acceptance as the "ideal" anchor. Below is a paradigm of those elements, outlining the "steps" an anchor must take to grow into the Command Anchor.

ANCHOR GROWTH PARADIGM

> **Level 5**—Trust: friendly, warm, comfortable, community asset, charisma

> **Level 4**—Recognition of Journalistic Skill: probes, digs, investigative, credible,expertise, knowledgeable, credentials

> **Level 3**—Style development: professionalism, naturalness, authoratativeness, credibility, interaction

> **Level 2**—Reading Skill: diction, delivery, clarity, speed, smoothness, interpretation

Level 1—Cosmetics: dress, make-up, appearnce, voice quality, gestures, mannerisms, body language

As you can see, cosmetic issues like make-up, dress, and appearance are basic to viewer acceptance. This is literally "the first step" that must be mastered if an anchor wants to be effective or considered "in command" of the newscast. In fact, if viewers don't like what they see, it is extremely difficult for them to get past their visual perceptions and actually listen to what is being said. The concept that one must master the first step of the paradigm before moving on can be termed the *succession rule*.

The succession rule holds true all the way up the paradigm. If one step is missed or not fully realized, the steps above, no matter how developed, are rendered "null and void" by the viewer. To illustrate this point, consider Level 5. Without the steps below Level 5, any television personality thought to be a "bubble-head" could just as easily also be considered friendly, warm, comfortable, charismatic, and a community asset. It is only when supported by the other four levels of the paradigm that those 5th-level characteristics become the highest facets of the Command Anchor. Taken a step further, if viewers have a choice between two anchors who possess the characteristics of levels 1–4, but only one of whom possesses the characteristics of Level 5, it's a safe bet that most viewers will choose the latter. The analogy would be choosing between medical doctors. Most people, given the choice between two doctors who have the exact same educational background and experience, would choose the doctor with the best bedside manner. As they say, "A spoonful of sugar helps the medicine go down!"

TECHNIQUES RUNDOWN

The Command Anchor is actually a Master Communicator with a specialty. As with the actor, the Command Anchor should utilize the basic concepts of Quality Core and the Human Condition as a foundation to build on. From that base, there are hundreds of tools and techniques the anchor can use to develop and strengthen the five levels of the Anchor Growth Paradigm. I have outlined what I consider to be the strongest of these elements in the following rundown.

LEVEL I: COSMETICS

Voice quality and appropriate body language are very subjective matters. In this case, what's good for the gander isn't necessarily good for his better half. It is prudent, when starting out, and periodically throughout one's career, to seek a professional "third eye" for advice and criticism. Listen to a coach and the viewers to gain perspective and to help you choose the best course of action for your particular image.

Occasionally I run into resistance on this subject based on the fact that the anchor does not want to be "turned into somebody else." The development at this level is not to make someone into someone else, but to bring out and capitalize on the best features that individual has to offer.

Consider turning on the news and being confronted by a street-bum sitting behind the desk delivering the news. I know it's an extreme example, but the old adage is true: "You don't have a second chance to make a good first impression." If the first visual images are disturbing or distracting, it is very difficult for the viewer to actually listen to what's being said. Although subjective, certain constants seem to hold true:

Visual communication trumps verbal communication.   No matter what is being said, the viewer will always first believe what they see. Visual images must match the verbal communication or the viewer is distracted. And remember, whether listening or talking, a person's body continues to communicate. Therefore:

Sit up and stay open.   Avoid crossing arms, clasping hands, and leaning on the desk. These gestures, used to an extreme, hinder expressiveness, look defensive and provide an obstacle between anchor and viewer.

Use your hands to communicate.   Every part of a person's body works in unison to communicate. If any part is left out, the entire unit suffers in its ability to communicate. If you were to sit on your hands to tell a story, your shoulders would naturally tighten a bit, your facial expressions would not be as animated, and your vocal range would decrease. As you do in normal conversation, use your hands. Even when the shot is so tight that your hands can't be seen, being expressive with your hands and body enriches your storytelling.

"The eyes are the windows to the soul."   As you finish a conversation with the viewer, on-set person, or "live" reporter, complete the thought before allowing your eyes to move to your copy. Your message will be stronger and you won't run the risk of seeming "dismissive."

Be careful of "prompter stare."   Normal conversations don't usually occur with both parties staring holes into one another. Your eyes will tell the viewer if you are really talking to them or at them.

Don't be trendy.   Be professional with clothing, jewelry and make-up. You want the viewers to see you as a professional community leader. In order to accomplish this goal you must dress appropriately.

Vocal Quality   The best vocal quality for a broadcaster has a base resonance and is well modulated. Intermittent, thin, high-pitched sounds are usually a product of inconsistent vocal placements and vowel formations. I'm a great believer in the power of positive thinking, but it has also been my experience that muscles rarely become stronger or tools of the will without exercise. Work with a voice coach for proper placement and clarity of articulation; a few hours each week with a coach and then on your own. The training and practice will make a tremendous difference in just a few months.

LEVEL 2: READING SKILL

As I mentioned earlier, no viewer, after watching a newscast, has ever exclaimed, "Great copy!" Viewers do, however, constantly state, in focus groups and polls, their strong affinity and need for conversational storytelling qualities from their anchors. Statements like, "...as if they were talking to me," "...that they seem interested in the stories they tell," and "...it should sound like they got the story" indicate that viewers want a great storyteller, not a mere reader.

Attention to storytelling or how a story should be delivered is a rarity. More often than not, anchors spend most pre-show preparation time doing myriad other things, such as rewriting scripts and editing video packages. These duties are important and must be accomplished, of course, but no time is set aside to work on the very aspect of a newscast vital to the viewer: copy interpretation.

On the other hand, anchors who make a concerted effort to be conversational and who communicate the Human Condition on a consistent basis are more likely to be regarded as fascinating and "in command." Here are a few suggestions to keep in mind as you aim toward better storytelling:

- *Prepare your copy*   Preparing copy is really a three-tiered process: Proofread to make sure spelling, grammar, and facts are correct. Study each story as a storyteller. Make notes and mark the script for the various emotional tones, coloration, and pacing found in each story. Practice by reading each story out loud, just as you will do it during the newscast.

- *Give the news to the one person who really cares*   To help interpret copy during prep-time, choose to tell a specific person who would most benefit from, or be moved by, each individual story.

If you tell it for that person's benefit, everyone will find it more interesting.

• *Emotional impact versus editorializing*   Lack of variety in hard news may come from a fear of editorializing. However, if a story is written in a balanced fashion and you are true to the words, you can tell the story with feeling and still be objective, and a lot more effective and memorable.

• *Monitor yourself to avoid the habit of always ending sentences with the same inflection*   Watch out for pattern emphasis of any sort that replaces conversational delivery. Meaningful conversation contains no repetitive patterns. All rhythm, inflection, and emphasis should be chosen based on their potential for enhancing the meaning of your message.

• *Pace versus rate*   Rate is the speed of delivery, how fast the anchors read. Pace is the ebb and flow of storytelling, including pauses, intense passages, and the full range of dramatic relief. Most anchors actually lose their pace when they push their reading speed past their natural limits. They also lose meaning, intensity, interpretation and emotional range. They swallow words; they skip periods. Use effective pauses and phrasing, and vary the tone of your stories.

• *Tone*   The single strongest vocal communicator is tone of voice. Analyze your copy to establish the basic mood of the story and then deliver it in the appropriate tone. You might find it especially helpful with hard news to write a descriptive adjective, i.e., compassionate, sardonic, somber, etc., to remind yourself during the newscast of what differentiates the stories. The thought process of picking the words can help you.

• *Emphasis*   There are many ways to get emphasis. One-word stress, while a perfectly acceptable form, is much used in on-air reading and the least used in natural conversation. Remember ours is a language of phrases, not "punching" single words.

• *Transitions*   Transitions are the road signs that keep the viewer with you. You need to add change of tone, pitch, or some other technique to emphasize them for the viewer.

- *Keep in mind the real reason for telling the story*   A story is not just about a flood, fire or shooting. It should be about the people involved. Find those words and phrases that help the viewer understand what the story is really about.

LEVEL 3: STYLE DEVELOPMENT

The presentation style viewers want most from an anchor is professional, authoritative, credible and natural. Being a great storyteller is just one device the anchor has to showcase those elements. Another tool the anchor has at his disposal is his credibility:

Don Shelby: My favorite communicator of all time is Reverend Dr. Martin Luther King, Jr. Not only was he a fabulous orator, he had a great deal to say. He had an audience that he cared about. He knew their needs, and he knew what they wanted to hear. And sometimes he told them what they wanted to hear and every once in a while he'd spend his credibility and tell them things they didn't want to hear.

You can bank credibility, but you can't buy with it. You gotta use it. It's not legal tender. You can gather credibility over a period of time, but it's of no value unless you use it from time to time. And every once in a while you've got to take that risk and you've got to say, "Now I've got to spend some of this credibility. I've got to ask people to have faith in me. I've got to ask them to use this stuff that they have invested in me and take that risk."

And so Martin Luther King, Jr. could say all he wanted to about civil rights and everybody wanted to hear that. But when he said the war was wrong, that was a shock to people. It sounded wrong, but they knew it was Martin Luther King, Jr. who was saying it, so they had to stop and pay attention to it because he was a man in whom they had invested a great amount of credibility. And as a result, his message resonated. And made people listen to the idea in a way they may have not listened to before. It was a seminal moment for me. I remember reacting negatively when he came out against the war in

Vietnam, sort of like, "That isn't any of his business! His business is civil rights!" But then it slapped me in the face. Of course it was his business. And as a man who demonstrated this huge public policy of morality, he might even be right. And so he took my listening into consideration. He knew I wouldn't like it.

And he said it anyway. So that's what I like about him. That he was willing to spend his credibility. That he was a fabulous orator. Chose his words well. He had great affection for his audience. And his message was the perfect message for the day.

Interaction is yet another significant tool the anchor possesses to produce such style. Interaction, or the communication between two or more individuals, can be used in various forms throughout the newscast. Many producers and anchors think of interaction as good for nothing more than "happy talk." To those individuals, interaction is a device used to make an easy transition from a news story to the weather segment, or a way to tease the viewers just before a commercial break.

Savvy newscasters use interaction to show responsiveness and context. The anchor's job is not only to deliver the news, but to put that news in context with everything else the viewer knows and understands about the world. When the anchor demonstrates an ability to react and respond to other anchors and reporters, it actually enriches the newscast. There are some considerations to keep in mind when adding interaction to the show:

- *Ideal Interaction*   There are seven basic elements that help make interaction appropriate and effective:

- *Ideal interaction is viewer centered*   It is distracting when anchors and on-set reporters become so involved with each other during interaction that they forget to include the viewer.

- *Ideal interaction adds information*   There are few things more aggravating to a viewer than a couple of anchors sitting around talking about nothing. It is a waste of precious time. Interaction should always add a new piece of information to the mix.

- *Ideal interaction reveals the anchor's character* By what an anchor says, how he or she communicates ideas and treats others, the viewer gets a pretty good idea of the anchor's true personality and core.

- *Ideal interaction highlights relationships* Interaction should reveal a genuine admiration and respect between colleagues.

- *Ideal interaction is concise* Keep it short and simple. Viewers are pretty sophisticated. If anchors continue to have a dialogue and don't continue to add new information, viewers become bored and tune out.

- *Ideal interaction is confident* Often the energy and volume levels fall when interaction occurs. This is usually due to the fact that the participants are not truly prepared, and therefore self-conscious because they are "winging it." For interaction to work well, it needs to have the same animation and intensity as the rest of the show.

- *Ideal interaction avoids one- or two-word affirmations* How many times after a report have we heard the anchor mutter, "Thanks John, great report!" while looking down at his script in transition to telling the next story? This kind of gratuitous response is nothing more than dismissive and does nothing to further the newscast.

- *Look for appropriate areas to inject interaction* Before the newscast, find areas in the show where interaction will work. There's no need to script what will be said, but do take time to discuss your ideas with the producer, weather and sports reporters, and co-anchor.

LEVEL 4: RECOGNITION OF JOURNALISTIC SKILL

I happened to be coaching an anchor team at a mid-western news station when their producer interrupted us to inform them of this story:

A twenty-eight-year-old man drove an expensive sports car toward a busy intersection near a residential section of town. He stopped for a red light, only to be lightly rear-ended by a senior citizen in a drop-top Cadillac. The old man had been paying insufficient attention to the road because of a rambunctious pet puppy dog sitting next to him. The younger man, obviously furious and distraught by the bump, pulled a revolver out of his glove compartment, jumped out of his car and bounded back, yelling at the old man still seated and now cowering behind the steering wheel of the Caddy. At that moment, a school bus full of kids approached, just in time to witness the crazed young man shoot the old man's yapping puppy. The screams of the shocked children startled their bus driver, who plowed into a telephone pole, injuring at least half of her elementary-aged passengers.

The producer then told the two anchors that they would be going live to a reporter at the scene, during their show. Without missing a beat, the anchors politely excused themselves from our session and bee-lined for the news-room. I followed and watched as they immediately grabbed the phones and started making calls. They contacted school officials, city officials, the police, and local storeowners. Within minutes, they had a stockpile of background information on the story: crime history of the area, the incidence of recent traffic accidents in that intersection, make-up of the neighborhood, safety records of local school bus drivers, etc.

That night, during the live report, those anchors preceded every question with information they had collected during those phone calls. They asked questions like, "The police chief told me earlier today that four gang-related shootings have occurred in that neighborhood alone in the last two months. Do we know if this shooter was a local gang member?" and "Those who belong to the PTA know that our bus drivers must be certified by the Red Cross in first-aid before they are allowed to drive a school bus. Do we know if this bus driver had to administer first-aid to any of the injured children?"

It was easy to see why this anchor team was number one in the market. The ability to say they had spoken to law enforcement officials upheld their credentials. The PTA information connected them to the community as ordinary folk interested in the well-being and safety of its children. The extra information about related crime stories in the area, and bus driver certification requirements, made the anchors appear knowledgeable and gave the viewers much-needed perspective. Ultimately, even if the viewer wasn't interested in that particular news story, by getting the story from these anchors, he obtained valued information about his community.

PERSPECTIVE

The suggestion that an anchor offer perspective during a newscast, or for a particular story, is sometimes met with resistance because many anchors equate perspective with bias. The fact is, offering perspective need not reflect the anchor's opinion in the least. Consider this definition of perspective:

Perspective:
The relationship of aspects of a subject to each other and to a whole.

Viewers want two things from the newscast: One element they consider vitally important is *content*. It is interesting to note, however, that viewers generally consider content to be similar (if not the same) on every local news channel. If that isn't bad enough, unless there is late-breaking news, viewers feel they have already gotten most of the content from the morning paper, their friends at work or on the car radio during the commute home.

The real reason viewers will choose to watch a particular station or a particular anchor is *perspective*. They not only want the content, they want to understand its importance in how it relates to other news items, their community, their family and their own personal lives. Without perspective, news is nothing more than data with little or no Human Condition.

Be their protector. Going that extra mile is what it's all about for the loyal, local news fan. They not only want someone who is going to give them the news, they want a *protector*. Think about your average viewers. They get up every morning, get dressed, get the kids ready for school, go to work, come home from work, get the kids ready for bed, wind down and go to sleep so they can start all over again the next morning. They don't have time to find out which schools are too dangerous for their kids, which neighborhoods are too hazardous to drive through, what they should watch out for as consumers, what the weather will be like in the morning, etc. They need their trusted anchors to *protect* them. And they will put their faith and loyalty in the anchors who show initiative as diggers and probers—demanding investigators who will ask reporters the tough questions and get the answers their viewers want to know.

Be their expert. A good, solid anchor knows enough about most subjects to ask intelligent questions and offer possible elements of perspective. The Command Anchor is not only well-read and worldly-wise, but excels to such a degree in two or three main interests that he becomes an expert in the viewer's mind.

> **For example:** Let's assume a Command Anchor has a strong affinity for children. That anchor will take a personal interest in every important children's story the station reports on, involve himself in special community services relating to children, promote and donate time and energy to organizations that help children, own the station's franchise[17] on children, and add perspective during the newscast any time a major story breaks regarding children.

As the Command Anchor has expertise in certain subjects, the anchors in a Command Anchor team complement one another by having different main interests. Together, they have expertise in the major areas of news: crime, health, consumer issues, children's issues, etc. Viewers automatically want to watch the Command Anchor team whenever a big story breaks, because they trust that not only will they receive the data, but they will also gain a better understanding and perspective about the subject and how it relates to their lives, their families and their community.

LEVEL 5: TRUST

We have already established that one must master Levels 1–4 before Level 5 can count as "icing on the cake" for the Command Anchor. Appearing friendly, warm and comfortable takes a certain amount of empathetic behavior. Over time, the anchor must understand and relate to the market to such a degree that he becomes an idealized representative of the local viewer: a kind of composite made up of all that is good about the viewers in that particular market. If the anchor does this on a consistent basis, viewers tend to have an affinity for him as they would for a friend or family member. Such a feeling is a powerful thing. So powerful in fact that for many viewers it is the basis of their loyalty. Consequently, if the anchor violates this special relationship it could mean an end to his career:

Sandra Connell: Many people have let foul language slip out on the air. There was a female anchor who had huge numbers, huge research scores, and was the darling of her market. Everyone loved her and she was at the number one station. One day she looked straight into the camera, during some technical problems, and said; "What the f*** is going on?" And although she apologized on the air and wrote an apology in the newspaper, she never recovered with the viewers. Ultimately, she left the business. To this day, people in focus groups make reference to that *faux pas*.

Obviously what she said on the air was unacceptable, but it didn't mean she was a different person. The viewers just saw a side they didn't know. Bottom line: real communicators have to be able to read their audience and still be themselves. We're capable of that. We start reading our parents practically from birth. By the time we hit our teen years, most of us have figured it out. It's instinct!

Thus, viewers harbor the same feelings for the Command Anchor that they might have for a favorite aunt or uncle everyone loves to invite to family get-togethers, because they are always interesting to listen to, fun to be around, and lighten up the room. But most importantly, because that anchor respects and reflects the viewer's trust.

Community Asset   At this point, the anchor is such an advocate for certain community issues that he becomes one of the market's experts regarding those issues. He not only keeps the viewers informed of those important subjects, but is also a major contributor to their betterment within the community. Therefore, the Command Anchor truly becomes a community asset.

Tortoise Or Hare

Once upon a time, Aesop's fabled race between the tortoise and the hare taught youngsters the maxim, "Slow and steady wins the race." With the advent of microwaves, cellular phones, personal computers and tanning booths, Aesop has been gutted, stuffed, and mounted next to vinyl records, slide rules and the dodo bird. Technology today affords us the opportunity to have what we want when we want it, at the touch of a button, with the speed of light. Unfortunately, the ability to gratify one's needs in an instant should be tempered with the knowledge that it doesn't come without a price. In the long run, a constant diet of "fast food" will sacrifice nutrition, nightly "chats" on the Internet will sacrifice the charm of face-to-face interaction, and climbing the career ladder too quickly without gaining a solid education and specific training in the field will sacrifice the ability to get past the craft of it and enjoy the art or spirit of it.

> *Lucy Himstedt:* Many producers and reporters who are starting out now days don't know how to write. They don't know grammar. That drives me crazy! And it's a Catch-22. You've got people at all levels now who don't appreciate grammar. I just don't understand that. But that's way before "J" school. That's grammar school. Somewhere along the way people are not being held accountable for learning the basics. Just basic subject-verb agreement. I went through this with a producer yesterday. "None of them have blah-blah-blah." And I said, "I don't think so!" All I did was point out the story and say, "There's a grammatical error, come back to me when you know what it is." He eventually found it. He took it off the AP wire by the way. And AP used to be a real stickler about that kind of thing. Of course, I'm not saying every story's going to be perfect. Don't let me throw that stone! I can see that ricocheting off the glass!
>
> There are basics you need to tell a story well. And I'm not only talking about grammar, I'm talking about basic math. Let's look at math. Think about how many stories you have to do on budgets for city councils! Think about the number of stories that have to do with statistics. You don't want to end up reading numbers, but if you don't

get them right then we wind up with misrepresentation.

Then there's geography. If they've just moved here I don't expect them to know every city in the state. But I'm talking about basic geography. "Where are the Dakotas? Point to them on the map. Didn't you know there were two? A north and a south?" I'm not kidding!

The best piece of advice I could give to a beginner is, "select a good school!" Find the best program in America for your major. If you can afford it and everything falls into place, that's where you should be. There are schools that have a great reputation for turning out some of the best television journalists in our business. The University of Missouri has its own television station that's a network affiliate and #1 in the market. Starting their junior year, those kids are running cameras, shooting and reporting stories, anchoring and producing shows. So when they graduate they know what they're doing and that they have chosen the right career.

Sandra Connell: Rather than someone who thought it was all glamour, and didn't even do an internship at a television station. It's a shame when someone invests four years of college to a degree that, in the end, they find out wasn't for them at all. It's a tough business. The deadline and crunch of "going live every day", isn't for everybody. It's hard for people to park their lives at the door. It doesn't matter how bad things are at home, or that you just wrecked your new car. You've got to put that behind you as if nothing happened. The audience can never know if you've had a bad day. Every day has to be a good day for your viewers, and that ability comes with practice and seasoning.

Lucy Himstedt: Troy State University, in Alabama, has a phenomenal program. They do daily newscasts like we do. They have deadlines. It's on cable. People see their newscasts. Their students walk in as interns and I consider that they are people who have already had their first job. I'm not teaching them how to edit or any of that basic stuff. Troy State is a well-kept secret.

Don Shelby: Do everybody a favor, including yourself: At the beginning of your career, go to the smallest market that will hire you. Work your butt off and do every job in the building. Get on the air as much as you possibly can, and make all of your foolish, stupid mistakes where they won't fire you or sue you, and the audience won't drag you kicking and screaming from the set. Most small markets are pretty facile at allowing those kinds of errors. They're pretty good about forgiving. They know they've got a market where young people are starting out, and they take a certain amount of pride in the fact that someday they see them in a larger market or on the network. So they allow you to make mistakes.

Also, in smaller markets you do everything. So when you get to the anchor desk in a big market, and a photographer comes up and says, "I couldn't get that shot," then you can say, "I can go get it for you!" or "If you want me to, I can show you how to get that shot." Or a producer says, "I couldn't make that edit." Then you say, "I can make that edit." The good anchor needs to be fully informed of everything going on around him. Got to know how to direct, got to know how to produce, got to know how to write, got to know how to report. You have to know it all. Doesn't mean you have to go out there and execute it, but you've got to know what's happening around you constantly so you don't feel like a victim up on the set being whipsawed with things completely out of your control. You will feel comfortable up there because you know what's going on.

There are many paths that lead to a career in broadcasting, and I'm certainly not here to tell you that getting a great academic education is necessarily the "right" path. There is no "right" path. One of the most successful network news anchors in our country today never finished high school. I would point out, however, that most of the masters at the top of the mark are highly motivated, highly skilled individuals. And that skill is a mix of natural talents supported by the blood, sweat and tears of concentrated, focused learning and training over a period of years. Whether the learning and training comes from an academic background, a mentor, or just plain self-assertion and actualization, the message here is that success does not come by osmosis, a *Deus Ex Machina* or the

Easter Bunny. Mastery is not a gift. A true master has earned the right to his title. And that knowledge gives him the freedom, the strength and the validation to retain it.

Quality Keys

- *Masters have Masters.* Great athletes and communicators know how to put their respect and trust into that one person who will lead/motivate them to success. They know how to listen, absorb, utilize and do.

- *It is possible to be unbiased and convey the Human Condition.*

- *The Command Anchor.* Viewers perceive the ideal anchor as "in command" of the newscast's content. The Command Anchor is the gracious host, the omniscient observer and the viewer's representative.

- *The Anchor Growth Model.* The paradigm of five levels or fundamentals an anchor must master in order to become dominant in the viewer's mind and in the viewer's acceptance as the "ideal" anchor.

- *The succession rule.* An anchor must master the first level of the Anchor Growth Model before moving on to the next level. If one level is missed or not fully realized, the levels above, no matter how developed, will be rendered "null and void" by the viewer.

- *Cosmetics.* Level 1 on the Anchor Growth Model. If the visual images are disturbing or distracting, it is very difficult for the viewer to actually listen to what's being said.

- *Body-language trumps verbal communication.* No matter what is being said, the viewer will always believe what they see.

- *Vocal Quality.* The best vocal quality for a broadcaster has a base resonance and is well modulated.

- *Reading skill.* Level 2 on the Anchor Growth Model. Viewers would rather the anchor be a great storyteller than a mere reader.

- *Style development.* Level 3 on the Anchor Growth Model. The style of presentation viewers want most from an anchor is professional, authoritative, credible, and natural. One significant tool the anchor possesses to produce such style is *interaction*.

- *Interaction*. Communication between two or more individuals. Savvy newscasters use interaction to show responsiveness and context.

- *Ideal interaction* adds information, is viewer centered, reveals the anchor's character, highlights relationships, is concise, is confident, and avoids one- or two-word affirmations.

- *Recognition of journalistic skill*. Level 4 on the Anchor Growth Model. The Command Anchor probes, digs, investigates, and is credible, expert, and knowledgeable.

- *Perspective*. The relationship of aspects of a subject to each other and to the whole. Perspective allows the viewer to understand the importance of a story by how it relates to other news items, the community, the viewer's family and personal life. Without perspective, news is nothing more than data without the Human Condition.

- *The protector*. Viewers want to put their faith and loyalty in the anchor who shows the initiative of being a demanding investigator. "The protector" asks reporters the tough questions and gets the answers their viewers want to know.

- *The expert*. The Command Anchor is not only well-read and worldly-wise, but excels to such a degree in two or three main interests, he becomes an expert in the viewer's mind.

- *Persona*. Level 5 on the Anchor Growth Model. The anchor must understand and relate to the market to such a degree that he becomes an idealized representative of the local viewer.

- *Community Asset*. An advocate for certain community issues, the Command Anchor keeps the viewers informed of those important subjects, and is a major contributor to their betterment within the community.

- *Mastery is not a gift*. True Masters earn the right to the title.

9 THE CROWD PLEASER

All right, class; it's time for a pop quiz. Take a look at the subjects below and tell me how they're related. You have thirty seconds. Go!

DEEP WATER	DOGS	FINANCIAL PROBLEMS
CANCER	LONELINESS	DEATH
FLYING	HEIGHTS	THUNDER STORMS
INSECTS	VOMITING	CONFINED SPACES

Literally thousands of phobias have been recorded over the years. If you said that the subjects above represent many of the fears people say they experience the most, you passed the test. Now if we were to come up with a list of the top-ten fears ranked in ascending order from least feared to most feared, the list would look something like this:

10. Dogs   9. Loneliness   8. Flying   7. Death   6. Sickness
5. Deep Water   4. Financial Problems   3. Insects and Bugs   2. Heights

And the number one phobia people rank as their worst fear?
1. Public Speaking!

As one famous comedian put it, what this list tells us is that most people who attend a funeral, if given a choice, would rather be in the coffin than delivering the eulogy.

Black humor to be sure, but not far from the truth. In various surveys conducted over the years, people ranked public speaking as their worst fear. So why do they aspire to doing it? Why do they gravitate to it like moths to a fire? The answer is simple: Power. The power to unlock minds. The power to touch souls. The power to capture hearts. People and nations are captivated, motivated and galvanize by the well-spoken leader. And as we have already seen, many of the most successful people in history have been fascinating public speakers. So whether you are an aspiring politician, religious leader, CEO, or trial lawyer; whether you want to speak to the nation, or your company, or a PTA meeting; this chapter's for you.

I was recently asked by a new client, a man who never in his life had the occasion to speak in front of a large group of people and who has suddenly been shoved into the national limelight, "What's the secret?"

"Excuse me," I said. This was, after all, our first meeting.

"It's important that I get my message across and that I don't look like an idiot." he said. "The president has a speaking coach. I know a CEO with a coach who is a wonderful speaker. What are they told? What's the real secret?"

Well here it is. For the first time in print I'm going to reveal the answer. If you want to be a commanding public speaker, this is all you will ever need to know —

THE REAL SECRET

Rhubarb. Eat rhubarb every day and you will be a great speaker. No? Well, you wanted an easy answer, so there it is. Rhubarb.

Okay, okay. So what's the *real* secret. What knowledge do those powerful speakers keep hidden from us mortals that makes them gods of the podium? What knowledge have they kept locked away in the vaults alongside the Warren Commission's actual findings and Area 51's space-ship? The truth is, *nothing*. There is no secret. There is no magic pill. The real truth, the simple truth, is that there are five basic elements that go into the make-up of a great public speaker. Not every person possesses them, and those who do don't necessarily live up to their potential. But without these five elements, a person can no more hope to be a consistently powerful communicator than he can hope to be the Superhero of Metropolis. And attempting to teach that person how to become a fascinating communicator is like trying to teach a pig how to sing. At the end of the day, all you can hope to achieve is a mean ulcer and a grumpy pig.

Disillusioned? Burst your bubble? Don't throw this book at the neighbor's howling dog quite yet. Most people actually have all of the five elements that are about to be revealed to you. Usually, the problem is not whether one possesses the necessary elements, but to what degree those elements exist and how willing the subject is to develop them. The elements, in no particular order, are:

DNA • Quality Core • Human Condition • Techniques • Practice

That's it. It's really that simple. Unfortunately, knowledge doesn't necessarily equate with possession or ability. Just because you know a thing doesn't mean you can do that thing. But it is a through-line that can lead us to our goal if we're willing to stay the course. So let's take a look at these elements for a better understanding of that course.

DNA

There are two schools of thought here: One is that *anyone* can be a great speaker; it just takes time and practice. The other school believes that the ability to command through oratory is inherent in the genes; one is either born with the ability or is not.

The scary truth? They're both right. No one has the power to wave a magic wand and endow another with a sense of humor or drama. No teacher, mentor, or genie can anoint a follower with the gift of rhythm and flair. What is possible, however is for the coach to help identify the talents and strengths of an individual's core, then offer ways to surface and develop those strengths and talents. Not everyone has the potential to be spectacular, but just about everyone has it in him to be good. And when it comes right down to it, "good" is all an audience really needs to appreciate, like, and respect the speaker. Yes, it is always nice to be "wowed" by the pyrotechnics of spectacle, but in the end, what audiences treasure is the feeling that they are walking away from a speech with something of value. There's an old saying that goes, "Don't let the perfect be the enemy of the good." Those who attempt perfection will always fail because perfection is relative, and therefore ephemeral. But striving to be the best you can be is not only real and attainable, it is desirable. Because "the best you" is unique to this universe. No one can do "you" better than you. And in turn, believing in that brings confidence. And that confidence is a powerful thing. Confidence quells nerves. Confidence makes the seemingly impossible, possible. If you think a thing difficult, it will be difficult. If you can visualize winning, you are well on your way to success.

TECHNIQUES

We have already discussed in great detail the concepts of Human Condition and Quality Core. These are the cornerstones from which one supports the tools and techniques of fascinating communication. And as evidenced in our discussions of actors and anchors, the set of techniques one uses is often particular to the venue, message, and type of communicator. For the public speaker, that set of techniques can be divided into two categories: preparation and delivery. The following discussion of these categories and their subsequent techniques is by no means unabridged. It is meant as a springboard for the development of your tools as a "good," dare I say, "great" public speaker.

PREPARATION

pre·pare: 1. To make ready, usually for a specific purpose; make suitable; train 2. To make receptive 3. To equip or furnish with necessary provisions, accessories, tools, etc. 4. To make oneself ready.

How sane is it to attempt riding a high-performance motorcycle in a world-class race when the only two-wheeled vehicle you've ever been on is a bicycle? How sane is it to attempt climbing Mount Everest when the only thing you've ever climbed out of is bed. And how sane is it to attempt speaking in front of a thousand people when the only speech you've ever given was for a make-up grade in a junior-high history class.

Granted, without the proper training and tools, failure to perform well in the first two examples could have tragic results. Then again, tragedy is relative. Giving a speech without proper preparation will at the very least be nerve-racking, and could very well be devastating.

> *Rick Dent*: I don't like shoot-from-the-hip events. Corporate and political clients are busy people, and they don't have time, and they don't want to put in the amount of preparedness that they need. If you're going out in public, you'd better be ready because you're not just giving a speech to a hundred people in a room. You're communicating to a couple hundred thousand. If you're in the Atlanta media market and you're on WSB, you're communicating to an audience of probably two million people. If you screw up you've made a massive mistake. And if they ever get popped with that one question that they're not expecting, and they stumble, then they have to spend a lot of money and a lot of man hours trying to clean it up.

So how does one prepare for a speaking engagement? The process can actually be broken down into four separate categories: audience, content, practice, and a pre-show-conditions checklist.

AUDIENCE

Recently a television network approached our company and asked that I coach the host of their nationally syndicated talk show, in hopes that it would help boost ratings. The network felt that the host was polarizing, and needed to learn how to appeal to "a wider audience base." In fact their own research showed that the target demographic (the type of people the network wants as the main audience for a particular show) didn't much care for the host, and in some instances would watch the show *in spite of* the host.

In reviewing a few of the past shows, it became apparent that the "host issue" was just the tip of the iceberg. It is true that the host needed to develop a better style and stronger interview techniques, but a much larger problem resided in the overall production. What many people inside and outside "the business" don't always realize is that the host does not work in a vacuum. The way a show is written, produced, and shot also has a great deal to do with how the host is perceived. In the case of this show, the host and production staff seemed to be creating a show that *they* liked. *They* found the guests interesting. *They* thought their jokes were funny. *They* appreciated the music and the clothes and the subjects discussed. What they neglected to do was to consider that the network's target audience might not embrace their sensibilities. In fact, viewers tuning in to that show felt like they had just crashed a stranger's party only to realize they had little in common with the host or the guests. The only difference is, finding a graceful exit at a boring party takes time. Blowing out of a television show that a viewer doesn't relate to takes one click of the remote.

The mistake is a common one. Whether creating a show or preparing a speech, most people begin by considering themselves first. If *they* were in the audience, what would *they* like to see and hear? What would *they* find interesting or funny? Many times this kind of thinking in the initial stages of preparation, because it tends to preempt all other considerations when making decisions regarding content, is the kiss of death. The fact is *they* are *not* in the audience and most likely *they* do *not* have the audience's sensibilities.

The first rule of thumb here is simply, *Think of the Audience First!* What would the audience like to see and hear? What would the audience find interesting or funny? The ultimate success or failure of a presentation will depend to a large extent on how completely and in what detail these three questions are answered regarding the audience:

1. Who are they?
2. Why did they come?
3. Why would they want to listen to me?

Who Are They?

When a speaker understands the audience, understands who they are, it is much easier to relate to them and to craft a presentation that is specifically designed for them. In turn, the audience will have much more affinity for the speaker and interest in the subject matter.

> *Rick Dent:* How can you develop a communication with people if you don't know culturally what is going on around you? How do you hang your hat on a message if you don't know what people are thinking or seeing or doing in the real world? It is so easy to connect with people you are trying to communicate with if you have some kind of hook culturally or something that's going on in their communities, or something that is going on in the state. And it doesn't have to be serious things. It can be funny things.

So what kind of information would be most helpful to know about an audience? To get the ball rolling, here is a basic checklist of subjects that should be researched and data that should be gathered:

Audience Information Checklist
Age Range
Education
Occupation
Gender
Marital Status
Children
Religion
Cultural Background
Hobbies / Activities
Interests

There are as many ways to gather information about an audience as there are audiences to address. What's important is not the method of collecting information, but what the speaker does with that information once it is accumulated. Obviously, not everyone in the audience will be the same age or have the same education or the same interests. In fact it is most likely that the larger the audience becomes the wider the range each statistic will grow. And as the numbers get bigger, so does the fear factor with many speakers. Just thinking about holding the attention of a large group of strangers with diverse interests, ages and backgrounds can be overwhelming.

The key word here is *strangers*. One major ingredient that causes fear in human beings is the unknown. Imagine for a moment finding yourself in an unfamiliar neighborhood, speaking to a stranger in a dark alley. Not a very comforting thought. Now imagine being in that same dark alley with a friend. The unfamiliar surroundings might still cause some nervousness, but it is possible to draw strength and comfort from knowing the person beside you.

Now let's magnify that concept. Imagine for a moment finding yourself in an unfamiliar building speaking to fifty strangers in a dimly lit room. (After careful consideration, one might choose being with the stranger in the alley.) Okay, imagine that same dimly lit room again, but this time speaking to a group of friends and family members. The thought still might cause a bit of angst, but certainly not as much as facing the complete unknown.

SUSIE Q.

If it is true that speaking to a friend is less nerve-racking than speaking to a stranger, then the same should hold true for a group of friends as opposed to a group of strangers. Consequently, it can be incredibly valuable for the speaker to take all the data gathered for each of the different character elements that make up the audience, come up with an average statistic for each element, and create a composite person or composite couple that represents the entire audience.

For instance: Let's say you have 100 people in the audience. From all the data gathered it is discovered that the audience ranges evenly in age from eighteen years old to fifty-four years old. Therefore, the average age of your audience is thirty-six. It is also discovered that ninety of the 100 audience members are women. Therefore the average gender is female. Out of those ninety women it is discovered that eighty-five work part-time jobs. So far, your composite person is a thirty-six-year-old woman who works part-time. And so on.

Crafting a speech or presentation for one specific person's (or one specific couple's) sensibilities is infinitely easier than doing so for the faceless masses. And because that composite character or composite couple comprises the average elements of the group, the content of the presentation will speak to most of the people most of the time.

Let's take, for example, the talk show that wanted help to increase the numbers of their target demographic. The first order of business was to ask the production staff and host for a description of their target demographic. Not surprisingly, no two people working on that show had the same notion of who they were supposed to be targeting. Next, I brought in a representative of the network so that together, we could all come up with a composite audience member that both network and staff would be comfortable targeting. The network's big concern was pulling in women aged twenty-five to fifty-four. After a few hours of looking at and discussing research data on this segment of the population, we came up with a composite audience member who looked something like this:

COMPOSITE AUDIENCE MEMBER

NAME: Susie Q.
AGE: 33
EDUCATION: 2–4 years of college.
OCCUPATION: Full time mother and housekeeper. Probably part-time, possibly full-time employment outside the home.
CHILDREN: Two kids: one pre-teen and one teenager.
MARITAL STATUS: Probably married. Possibly divorced.
RELIGION: Practices faith based on God. Christian or Jewish.
CULTURAL BACKGROUND: Roots vary. Second- or third-generation American.
INTERESTS: Kids, health issues, cooking, bargains, consumer issues, saving money, cosmetics, school issues, clothes / styles, time management, vacations, household products, Hollywood news, etc.
HOBBIES / ACTIVITIES: Crafts, gardening, exercise, biking, school functions, etc.

Once the talk show staffers had a clear understanding of their target audience, they approached their jobs differently. The kinds of guests that were booked and the material written for the host changed to become more "Susie-friendly." In fact, every time a staffer came up with a new idea, the first question asked was, "Would Susie like it?" The same shift in attitude and style held true for the host's sense of humor and interviews. The content of both was now geared more toward Susie's sensibilities.

(Rick Dent) You'll find, especially in the Deep South, almost all statewide contests now will start out 42 percent to 42 percent. That's pretty much where the democrats are and the republicans are. So in a sense, every election is decided by that group in the middle, that ten-to-sixteen-percent in the middle. And they're not motivated by anything but pragmatism. What they care about is getting the job done. They're pragmatists. If republicans can do the job they'll vote for republicans. Which explains why in 1994 you had this sweep in the Deep South of republicans everywhere. But by 1998 those same people decided, "Well those republicans really didn't do the job, did they." And they switched back to the democrats. And I think you're going to keep seeing that. They're going to throw out who doesn't get the job done. They just want the job done.

Now they will not support an extremist in either party. They're going to reject a democrat who they perceive as too liberal. But we're still talking about the same basic message. If you're too liberal, it means you're not dealing with the things that matter to me. If you're too conservative your not dealing with matters that I care about. And it's really about that great meld.

And psychologically, for the speaker, making the presentation becomes that much easier when embracing the idea that the audience is made up of people who have all the same characteristics, needs and desires.

WHY DID THEY COME?

Is the audience there to be entertained? Informed? Motivated? Are they there to laugh? To grieve? The answer to this question will guide the content, suggest the style, and color every aspect of the speaker's presentation.

WHY WOULD THEY WANT TO LISTEN TO ME?

Based on the Composite Audience Member information what qualities, qualifications, characteristics and so on does the speaker have in common with the audience? What can the speaker offer—that he personally identifies with—that would be of value to the listener? And speaking from first-hand experience is ultimately easier and sounds more heartfelt than manufacturing examples and stories.

THE MESSAGE

After getting a handle on who the audience will be, the next step in the speaker's preparation is dealing with the content of the speech. What will be the core issue? How does that issue relate to the audience? And what will be the ultimate goal or goals of the presentation?

> *Rick Dent:* It's been the trend starting in the early '90s. Clinton capitalized on it but he didn't invent it cause people were already doing it. It's this concept of whatever it is you're talking about, make sure that it relates to the daily lives of the voters. They don't care about political games. They have positions on the social issues like abortion and prayer in school, and they certainly like to know where you stand on those. But when they're at home, after they've put their kids to bed and they're sitting at their kitchen table, they're not talking about prayer in school and they're not talking about abortion rights. They're talking about whether they're kid goes to a decent school or not. Whether that school is safe. Whether there are drugs in that school. Whether their community is safe from violence. Whether there is so much traffic that it's a pain in the ass to get to work. Those are the kinds of issues that impact their daily lives. And if you are a politician and can communicate both your sensitivity to those issues and actually have something to offer, they'll vote for you. But you've got to relate to their lives. Communicate to what that person cares about as opposed to what you care about and you gain their trust.
>
> And if you get that trust, whatever office you have, whether it's the US Senate or Governor or the President, if you wonder away from that agenda or those issues that impact there daily lives and get into

crap, you'll hear about it and you'll be hurt. The classic example that everybody can relate to was Bill Clinton in 1992. Certainly with, "I feel your pain" and "It's the economy stupid," he related to the middle class that had almost all but been forgotten. That's what got him elected.

Then as soon as he got elected, what did he do? He basically said to America, "What's important to me right now is gays in the military." Well, people went nuts. Sure you've got some people that are opposed to that. But by and large there was a cultural disconnect. "We didn't vote for you to go to Washington to deal with Gays in the military. We voted for you because of the economy!" And he got slammed for it. And that happens way too often.

That's all it is. If people think you care about the same things, that's how they bond with you. And then they believe you'll do the right thing when it comes to the policies. Because, "You think like me." You understand what it's like to get those kids to daycare at 7:30 in the morning and then run to work. You understand there's drugs in my kid's school, cause you've got kids.

CORE ISSUE

An audience will not walk away from a speech having memorized everything that has just been presented to them. In fact, within hours they will probably forget 80 percent of what they heard. What they will remember is a concept and possibly a couple of key points. So the speaker should begin crafting the message by deciding what the core issue will be, and the two or three main points to support that issue. Everything else in the body of the presentation should be fashioned to support the core issue and those main points.

DOES THE AUDIENCE REALLY CARE?

After deciding on a core issue, ask yourself if the audience really cares. Does it interest them? Does it add value to their lives? After deciding on the two or three main points that will be presented to support the issue, do the same. This question should be applied to every aspect of the speaker's content. Yes, it is probably true that no matter what the speaker says or does, there will be *someone* in the audience who relates. The point is, however, if the speaker does not relate to *most* of the audience *most* of the time, the presentation will not be as successful or powerful as possible. So keep asking the question!

GOALS

Here is a saying that is worth repeating and remembering:

> *Don't let the perfect be the enemy of the good.*

The speaker who wants everyone in the audience to like him will fail. The speaker who needs everyone in the audience to believe in everything that he says will fail. The speaker who strives to give "the perfect speech" will fail. Abraham Lincoln said it best:

"It is true that you may fool all the people some of the time; you can even fool some of the people all of the time; but you can't fool all of the people all the time."

Striving for perfection only produces anxiety, because perfection is not possible for most of us mere mortals. And attempting that unattainable goal in front of a group of strangers will make the experience that much more stressful and anxiety-ridden for the presenter. Striving to be a good, solid speaker by giving the audience something of value is not only possible, it is entirely attainable.

As a successful songwriter, musician, singer and producer, Gary Chapman is a Grammy Award-nominated performer who has also won recognition in contemporary Christian music circles as Gospel Music Association's "Male Vocalist of the Year." Gary has also written hits for many artists, including Alabama, Kenny Rogers, Vanessa Williams, and Amy Grant. His song, "Finally," was a #1 Country hit for T. G. Sheppard. As a recording artist, Chapman received the 1996 Dove Awards for "Male Vocalist of the Year," "Inspirational Recorded Song of the Year" and "Special Event Album of the Year." Most recently, Gary became permanent host of The Nashville Network's (TNN) flagship music/talk show, *Prime Time Country*. In this venue, his skills as an interviewer are right on par with his other, already proven talents, and are matched by his quick wit and humor, which garnered him a 1997 *Music City News* Country Award as "Comedian of the Year."

Gary Chapman: There is a place in singing that I have naturally been able to find that I credit to my mother to a large degree. And that is the ability to be lost in a song. It's a detachment from the audience that the audience so appreciates. To see you lose yourself in that work. I don't know if you can teach that. It is simultaneously lonely and embracing. To walk out on that ledge in front of a group of people... you're on the ledge by yourself, but you're in the predicament with everybody. And learning how to trust the fact that if you fall, it's okay.

Learning to know that that is always going to be the case is the next level for me as a talk-show host. I trust that it's there sometimes, I don't trust that it's there all the time. Getting to the point where you don't care if it works or not, tends to make it work. It's like so much of life. And I don't know why I have to learn this lesson again and again and again. If I'm in a position where I know my natural gifts are there, the harder I try, the harder it is and the less positive results I get. The less I try, the more I relax and the more positive results I get. And it's just a very interesting irony. And it is the case for me.

Being willing to fail is everything. To enjoy the risk and know that you get to wake up tomorrow and try again. I don't know why it's taken thirty-nine years to really embrace that concept...to just let go. To just let go! I think after thirty-nine years of holding stuff, my arms finally gave out. I'm serious. That's what happened. I finally said, "I just can't do this any more! And for my own health, I'm gonna let go!" And you know, the wild thing is, most of the stuff I have historically held on to, dropped and stayed. The great things that I really wanted in the first place, they bounce. And they're suddenly back in your sight again. And you go, "Oh, look at that!" Of course, then the danger is to grab it again. I think you should just dribble those things. You shouldn't ever hold them. That's "traveling." And you will be penalized.

Since the speaker has no control over what the audience will do, his goals should be based on the concept of giving to the audience instead of taking from the audience. The only known factor is what he can produce for his auditors, not what their reaction will be. Keeping the attention on ways to inform, persuade and entertain will produce a higher rate of success than looking for acceptance and love.

> *Bill Taylor:* You have to care yet care not. We tend to want to please everybody but you simply can't please everybody. Life is a battle-ground. You have to be in the care-not stage. "I don't care what you think!" And while that sounds harsh, there's truth to it. After all, that's what television programs do, that's what everything does today. Everything is fragmented and segmented to "I don't care if you don't like me. If you're not interested in this, don't buy it. Don't watch it, don't buy it, don't go to the movie." That's why we have this variety of life today. The variety almost fatigues us there's so much of it anymore.

NUTS AND BOLTS

I know what you're thinking, "All right, all right! I know who my audience is and I promise not to base my self-worth on their reactions. Can I please write my speech already?"

And my answer to you would be, "No!" Well, actually "Yes and no." This *is* the point in preparation where the idea needs to meet the written word. A speech or presentation should be put into outline form so that the full structure is on paper. At that point, many speakers consider their preparation complete. And those are the speakers who usually look nervous and unprepared when presenting that material. Furthermore, a speaker's total reliance on a full speech written out word for word takes away his control and gives all of his power to that stack of papers. This forces the speaker to be nothing more than a reader for his audience instead of a speaker to his audience. Audiences do not want someone reading to them. They can read for themselves. What they appreciate is a good storyteller. What they have affinity for is a speaker who has affinity for them.

> *Rick Dent:* Number one: know your remarks. Don't sit up there and read. Actually spend time with the language. Spend time on what it

is you want to communicate. Keep it short and simple. But know it!
The more you know it the more comfortable you will appear and the
more people will like you.

THE RULE OF THREES

People tend to identify with and have affinity for words, phrases, and
concepts that are grouped in threes. This is not scientific. I have no
empirical data to back this statement up. But it is, nevertheless, true.
Consider so many of the phrases we hear on a daily basis:

"Morning, noon and night."
"Ready, set, go!"
"Breakfast, lunch and dinner."
"Friends, Romans, countrymen..."
"The pope, the president and Dolly Parton walk into a bar..."

This rule of threes is a simple yet powerful device that can be applied
to every aspect of the presentation. For instance:

Beginning, middle and end   Breaking down the speech into three distinct sections makes it easier on the speaker when crafting a presentation.
The first part should include a statement of welcome and an overview.
Some speakers will also use this opportunity to ask a question or tell a
story, but hold off on giving the audience an answer to the question or
wrapping up the tale until the end of the presentation.

The three "G's"   Tell them where they're *going. Go* there. Tell them where
they've *gone.* It's the simplest of all the three-rule concepts but one of the
most powerful. In the beginning, tell the audience what they are about
to experience. Give them that experience. And when it's done, review.

Deliver the message in threes.   A presentation should have one major
goal or message that can be divided into three parts for the audience:
Today we will learn how to re-paper your bathroom in three easy steps:
preparation, application, and cleanup.

Deliver concepts in threes.   Another simple, yet powerful tool: Each main point or concept that is introduced in the body of a presentation can be made more dynamic by the rule of threes. Take for instance John F. Kennedy's inaugural address in 1961:

> "And so, my fellow Americans, ask not what your country can do for you, ask what you can do for your country. My fellow citizens of the world, ask not what America will do for you, but what together we can do for the freedom of man. Finally, whether you are citizens of America or citizens of the world, ask of us here the same high standards of strength and sacrifice which we ask of you."

Or Abraham Lincoln's Gettysburg address:

> "That this nation, under God, shall have a new birth of freedom, and that government of the people, by the people, for the people, shall not perish from the earth."

Communicate the Human Condition by Using Your Quality Core

Simply put, don't say anything you can't wrap your core around. More often than not, if a speaker communicates something he's not comfortable with, the audience will feel it, sense it or know it.

> *Rick Dent:* America will forgive almost anything. What they don't forgive is lying. They hate liars. And a lot of times you'll see a politician make a mistake and then compound it by lying or hiding information about it. And that's usually where the damage occurs. Not in what you originally did but how you handled it afterwards.
>
> What you find both in government and in corporations is that you run into attorneys. Attorneys don't believe in openness. They don't believe in truthfulness because they think that gets you into trouble. So you always have this natural clash between the public relations side and the legal side. Any crisis, whether it is something that's going to hurt your company, or a candidate just screwed up, or a state agency just screwed up, it's really about rapid response. If

there's a crisis that breaks, Number one: you need to do your own in-house investigation to find out what the facts are. That does not mean a four-month investigation; that means a two-hour investigation. Find out what the facts are *now*. Number two: it means having a corporate culture or a political culture where people are actually honest internally. I can't tell you the number of times in the middle of a crisis you can ask a staff member a question and they will give you the answer they think you want to hear. As opposed to the truth. Because they think they're actually helping you. And that is not the case. Your not trying to point fingers, you just need to know what the facts are. Number three: get the facts out as fast as possible. Even the facts the media may not know yet. And then number four: fix it. It's really that simple.

WRITE LESS TO READ LONG

A speaker should never go over his allotted time. It only alienates him from his audience. The best speakers plan on finishing early. When a speaker tries to cram too much information into a time allotment, the natural inclination is to rush. The best speakers pad their presentations by crafting only enough material to fill 90 percent of the allotted time. This allows time for questions, or gaffes, or just speaking naturally.

BULLET POINTS

A well-written script will embody every dynamic, facet, and nuance in narrative form. One approach to help the speaker deliver that material in a conversational fashion is to boil it down into outline form or bullet points, and use only those as guideposts instead of reading the full script during the presentation. This method eliminates the possibility of reading at the audience, and forces the presenter to speak directly to the audience.

PRACTICE

Think back to the time when you first learned how to drive a car or ride a bike. In both instances, you were probably so focused on the mechanics of operating the vehicle—the exact position of your hands, the amount of pressure applied by your feet, the indications of the instruments, or the position of your body—that you couldn't concentrate on anything outside your immediate surroundings, or see more than thirty feet in front of you. But with each time you practiced you became more familiar with the vehicle and the skills necessary to operate it, which helped you to become more relaxed, which, in turn, allowed you to forget the mechanics and take in more of your surroundings. And today when you ride that bike or drive that car, you don't think twice about your performance. You let your subconscious control the physical operation while you focus most of your concentration on what's happening around you and where you're going.

As a coach, one of the hardest things to do is to get people to practice. Maybe it's the time factor or the idea that everything in today's world should be instantaneous, but many clients have it in their heads that simply knowing the information is enough and that it will somehow seep into their core being and immediately be translated into their work. *Wrong!*

> *Bill Taylor:* Just like team sports in high school, the coach said "practice, practice, practice!" No matter what you want to do in life, and particularly for a communicator, to do it well takes a great deal of practice and therefore discipline. There are those who have natural abilities, who don't think they have to practice or prep or enhance those abilities. And that's just foolish. Doctors, lawyers, teachers, dentists, all of these professionals go back to school regularly and have to be either re-certified or get additional training because there is wisdom to that. The best communicators are people who practice a great deal. Who have the ability to look at themselves, to put a video tape into a machine, to look at a movie, to look at a tape of their speech that they gave, or their interaction in sales or whatever it might be, and say, "I hate watching this but I see what I do right and identify what I'm not doing so well." And then work at fixing it. You know the old saying, "Anything worth doing is worth doing well." It's about being an achiever. It's about practice.

Practice possible questions and answers. They don't have to memorize any given answer. Maybe on the more difficult questions, if there's a controversy and you want to get it just right, then yes. Practiced answers are about theme and message and the kinds of points you want to make. Go through a role-playing of every conceivable question and every conceivable answer. Get that down and then go out and hold your breath and keep your fingers crossed. And it's okay if you get popped with a question you don't know the answer to. Just say "I don't know the answer." It's much better to say I don't know the answer than it is to screw up and make a big mistake. "I don't know the answer but I can find out the answer and get back with you."

> *Rick Dent:* People never even think about that. All these folks want to pretend like they know all the answers, and that's why they are the corporate CEO or that's why they are the governor or the U.S. senator. You'd be surprised how receptive a group of voters can be when they actually see someone who says "I don't know but I'll find out."

Practice is 80 percent of the battle. Just like driving a car, the more you practice, the more familiar you are with the material, the easier it will be to pay less attention to the written words and more attention to speaking in a conversational manner directly to your audience. And don't fool yourself into thinking that practice means "running it in my head." For the body and spirit to get comfortable with an action, they must physically do that action again and again. The most confident speakers actually stand and vocalize their presentation, running it repetitively until it becomes second nature. A few more practice tips:

- *Practice in front of a real-live audience* You don't necessarily need the feedback or criticisms of family and friends, but it's helpful to practice in front of warm bodies. Get the feeling of looking into their faces and gauging delivery off of their reactions.

- *Eye contact* Whether rehearsals are done in front of people or a wall, practicing eye contact is essential. Run the speech enough so that only an outline or bullet points on index cards are necessary to deliver the presentation. Ninety percent of a speech should be delivered by looking into the faces of the audience, not the script.

• *Tape and study practice sessions*   Record each rehearsal on video
or audio tape. Review practice tapes to identify strengths and
weaknesses, then use that knowledge during the next practice
session, building on the positives and eradicating the negatives.

Odds and Ends

Assuming that your preparation is complete, you know your audience,
you have your presentation down cold, you're a walking, talking, pub-
lic-speaking maniac hyped and ready for action; there are still a couple
of issues that should be addressed before the event takes place, just to
make sure things run smoothly.

• *Appropriate dress*   There's nothing worse than arriving at a costume party dressed as a Hershey's Kiss, only to realize that you
must have looked at the wrong invitation as you make your grand
entrance into a black-tie affair (a story recently told to me by a
client). Remembering that the first impression is a lasting one,
what the speaker wears is the audience's first indication of what
they will be experiencing.

Rick Dent: It's a double-edged sword. If you look natural in your
choice of clothes, you get votes. If you look like you're conde-
scending and unnatural and you look phony, it will gut you.
It's real easy when you work with a lot of politicians to get really cynical. You see all their foibles internally. And you forget
sometimes that a governor or a lieutenant governor or an attor-
ney general or a U.S senator, when he goes into a town, it's still
big doings. You see the way people react. They get excited because these people are important. And they want you to look a
certain way and it's real easy to undercut that if you're not careful. They want you to look like the kind of representative that
they want, even if you don't look like them. So you can run the
risk of looking like a phony if your not careful. I tell folks not to
pretend. If you are comfortable in blue jeans and a plaid shirt,

then wear it and you will look comfortable. If you're pretending to be comfortable in a pair of jeans for the camera, it will show. And you know it will show. Don't pretend to be something that you're not because people will spot a phony a mile away.

• *Arrive early*   Go to a speaking engagement early enough to check the equipment and surroundings, giving yourself plenty of time to rearrange things and fix problems if they exist.

• *Equipment*   Remember to check the sound equipment and sound levels. Make sure the lighting gives the proper mood and allows everyone to see you clearly. If your presentation includes the use of audio/visual equipment, practice with it to make sure it runs properly. Make sure you have enough of everything: chalk, markers, paper, materials, handouts, etc.

• *Surroundings*   If necessary, rearrange the surroundings to create the optimum atmosphere for you and your audience. Is the seating arranged for the best visibility? Is the room at the proper temperature? Are there any distractions that should be dealt with before your audience arrives? Do you have what you need at your fingertips for a smooth presentation: index cards, water pitcher and glass, microphone, etc.?

• *Rehearse*   Once everything is set, give yourself enough time to physically and vocally run through portions of your speech. The more you practice in the actual venue, the more relaxed you will be for the presentation.

THE INTRODUCTION

The day has finally arrived. You've done your homework and know your audience cold. You've written and rewritten your speech, honing it to razor-like sharpness. You've practiced in front of friends and family so many times, *they* could do the presentation. You arrived at the venue early enough to check and recheck everything, rehearse and re-rehearse everything, with enough time left over to build Rome. Dressed to the nines and feeling like the cat that ate the canary, you beam as the audience pours into the seats you so carefully rearranged for their optimum seeing and listening pleasure. You think to yourself, *I could die right now and be happy.*

The host rises and addresses the audience. Just a few words of welcome before introducing "the main speaker for today." He says something charming and the audience laughs.

You think to yourself, *Good! Get them warmed up and ready for the kill.*

The host gestures in your direction while still holding the crowd in the palm of his hand. He introduces you by saying, "And now, without further ado, here's ah...ah..." He then picks up a torn sheet of scratch paper with something scribbled on it that he can't quite make out, and squints at it while mumbling, "Uh...is that Alan or Alvin? I'm sorry I can't make this out." The crowd rustles in their chairs as your Garden of Eden begins to wilt. The host looks up and makes a joke to cover the *faux pas*: "Well, I hope *his* notes are *better* than *mine!*" The audience laughs uneasily, beginning to feel that they might be no more than unsuspecting cattle being led to Steak City.

You make your way to the podium under the scrutiny of glaring eyes. A cold sweat breaks out all over your body, and you think to yourself, *I wish I could die right now, and then I would be happy.*

Bill Taylor: For a speaker, the introduction and set-up are terribly important. They give the audience a framework in which to accept the speaker's information and style, to accept his importance and knowledge. That perspective gives the audience the ability to judge him as a fascinating communicator.

Being captivated by somebody often doesn't happen at the very first moment. Whether you watch someone on television or in a movie or see someone speak, it's important that you have some perspective. You have to get acquainted with them. Yes, there is that first impression about a person. Yet, often those first impressions are changeable as you get to know more about a person. We all make those snap judgments and categorize people. It's unfortunate because it's really restrictive. But typically, getting acquainted with somebody through someone else's perspective can change all that.

Many speakers tend to forget that the introduction is a vital part of the presentation. The right introduction will "warm up" the audience and predispose them to the speaker's subject matter or style. The wrong introduction can dig a hole so deep as to become the speaker's grave.

"So what am I supposed to do," you ask, "*write my own introduction?*"

And the answer of course is, "*yes!*" If the host doesn't know you, or even if he does, write out what you feel will best jump-start the event. Make the introduction pertinent to the presentation. It should emphasize your credentials and suggest your style. Remember the Three G's Rule? First things first. *Tell them where they are going.* In the case of the introduction, the audience should be thrilled that they will be going there with you.

IN THE BEGINNING

The initial part of a speaker's presentation should set the mood and rhythm for his listeners. This is the "honeymoon period" when the audience gets a feel for who the speaker is and what the speaker is about. And, just as important, it is the speaker's opportunity to get a read on his audience.

Don Shelby: There are two elements of communication that interest me. One is the ability to form a message and to present it in a way that the audience, whether it's one person or a million, receive it in exactly the way it was intended. With no mistakes, with all of the persuasion and emotion that the message carries at its outset. That it is received intact. The second part of the communication process is the listening process. If you are going to be a communicator, you've got to get your audience in a position to listen comfortably to what you're saying. And most people don't take that into consideration. The listening part. They take the message part very seriously. And they form their messages in a way that they think is cohesive or persuasive. But they do not take into consideration the condition or the mind-set of the person who is going to be absorbing the information.

You can communicate effectively in hundreds of different ways, and we have hundreds of different styles of great communicators

out there. But to me, the success comes from an accurate understanding and assessment of the audience, and framing your message
with them in mind. Not with you in mind. Otherwise you're just
speechifying. But if you really care that the individual, or the
individuals, to whom you are speaking, comes away from that
moment with the information intact, you've got to spend a great
deal of time thinking about them. And the best people who do
that are the ones who seem to have a feeling for and an understanding for their audience.

I've spent some time with an organization that is little known to
most people. It's called the ILA, the International Listening Association. It is an actual group of people. I was asked to give a speech to
this group. They were the ones who first introduced me to the concept of listening as being 50 percent of the communication process.
When they listen, they are frightening.

When I stood up to give the speech, after about a minute, I
noticed that this audience was, in fact, listening to me. Not pretending to be listening, not vacuous vacant eyes. But people who were
absorbed. People who were making themselves listen and be absorbed with what I was saying. So it really didn't depend on how
well I speechified. Because they were taking full advantage of their
resources. Of listening. And to do that properly, they explained, you
have to do something that we don't do naturally. And that is you have
to set aside your own ideas about what's being said. You can not race
ahead and form an argument thinking, "Here's what I'm going to say
in response to this person."

What happens is, after you've said something to a person who is
a terrific listener, there is silence for a period of time as the person
now, at the conclusion of the message, begins to think what they
should say. As opposed to thinking what they should say as it's being
said. ILA gave me that. So what I have done is become a better
listener. And as I become a better listener, I have become better
attuned to watching the faces of people, as I speak. And if I'm
making my point, I'm okay. But I can tell by their faces if I am or not.
Then I have to do something to get their attention once again. Just
the idea of knowing that I'm only in charge of 50 percent of the

communication process has been a helpful device to make sure I'm taking everybody into account when I'm talking.

There is no need to "wow" the crowd in the first few moments. In most cases the audience comes prepared to listen and wants the speaker to win. And as long as the speaker is invested, fervent, and remains genuine, the audience will be supportive. If the speaker feels honored by the invitation to make the presentation, he should say so. And the speaker should never begin with a joke unless he or she has the skills and experience of a professional standup comedian. It is important to have a sense of humor throughout the presentation, but telling a joke at the outset of a big speech is like going to Las Vegas for a two-week vacation and betting everything you own the first moment you walk off the plane. Chances are you'll lose. And if you do, the rest of the vacation will seem like an eternity.

> *Rick Dent:* It is much harder to coach a political candidate to have humor than it is to be serious because many times you'll find that they have no personal rhythm. Don Siegelman (Governor of Alabama) has no rhythm at all. I've always written his major speeches for him. I come from the Deep South where there's a rhythm. If I was influenced, I was influenced by a Black minister. I believe there is a rhythm to the way you say words. He can't say it to save his life. And humor is tough for him as well because humor demands a certain kind of rhythm. A certain kind of take. Anyone can be indignant and passionate. You can fake that. It's hard to fake funny.
>
> With some politicians, you just have to pull the plug and say that they're not funny. And just stay away from it. Sometimes that's the hardest thing to do, to tell someone "It's just not worth it," or "You just won't be able to pull it off." And the worse thing in the world is to try and be funny and not be. That's just awful. You feel for the person who's trying to be funny; you feel for the audience who all of a sudden gets really uncomfortable. If they think you're just bullshitting them with seriousness, they can handle that. But boy do they hate someone who's not funny. It's just a question of rhythm and getting comfortable with the material. Practice makes perfect. And if they ever go out there and get a laugh, the next time it's a lot easier. But

it's scary for anybody to stand up in front of a group of people and tell a joke and it not be funny.

The easiest is jokes at their own expense. That's much easier than to sit up there and to try to make a point with a joke. And it works in two ways. Number one: It's easier to make fun of yourself than to tell a joke 'cause it's more natural. Number two: I think people are sick to death of corporate CEOs and politicians who think too much of themselves and are too serious. I'm sick and tired of these blow-dried perfect candidates and I really think in the next five or ten years the candidates who really succeed will be the antithesis of that. Regular natural folks who speak their mind, who speak honestly and don't look like they're over-prepared and afraid to answer questions.

Bill Taylor: A rule of thumb would be, "Don't take yourself seriously but take your business seriously." Humor is a great antidote for the tension of business today. Now it can also backfire on you because not all of us have the same sense of humor. Sarcasm is never appropriate, although humor will occasionally bite like that and you have to be careful. But humor is one of those things that needs to be used a lot in business because it takes the edge off of things. It takes the serious-ness off of the dealings with each other and interjects a human element. Having fun even when the work is hard is a reasonable goal. There's nothing greater than a good laugh. Or even a great smile can break the tension in a room so that you can move on to another level. The goal is to be effective. The goal is to make things happen. The goal is to communicate. Humor helps and it should be used with regularity. Humor also allows you to disclose part of your personality to people, allowing a client or a college to feel more simpatico with you, more at ease. Then they're able to express themselves because you've used humor to open yourself up to them.

Back to our "Three G's Rule" once again, the first section of a speaker's presentation tells the audience where they will be going. Many experi-enced presenters will use a short dramatic story or a quote or a shocking statistic at this point to grab the attention of their audience. One such speaker is Terry Jones, president of SABRE Interactive and CEO of The

SABRE Group, a world leader in the electronic distribution of travel and travel-related services utilizing consumer-direct, online travel-planning sites like *Travelocity*, which has sold more than 2.5 million airline tickets to date, registered more than four million members, and logged more than 55 million page views per month.

Terry Jones: I had never really done any speaking until I came to work for SABRE. All of a sudden I had to go around the country and speak to travel agents, usually 500 at a crack, about what products we were bringing out and try to get them excited about staying with the system.

At first I was thrust into it and it was kind of scary. I would decide what I had to present, figure out how to say it and inject some excitement and some humor into it and make it real for these people. It became fun because it was different than the rest of my job and I found I really enjoyed doing it.

You absolutely have to know your stuff cold. Also, whatever good reviews I've gotten are from people who've said, "You can talk about technology in ways that I can understand." I try to not be technical but talk to them in terms of their business. And that's relatively easy for me because I was a travel agent years before I was talking to travel agents. I knew their business. I had been where they were.

People are afraid of technology. They don't know what it is. And technology ought to be transparent. You don't need to teach people how to run the Hoover dam to turn on a light bulb. Most people don't understand the functioning of an internal combustion engine but they drive cars. So if you can just make it simple for people and make the technology go away, that's a key.

I talk to them in terms of their reality and how these tools can improve their reality. And talking to them in business terms or cultural terms. At some point you have to talk to them about bits and bites but you can make it fun. And particularly if you can inject humor and empathize with the kinds of problems they have and to start out a presentation by talking to them about the crazy things that have happened to them in their jobs. We have a help line, and to mention some of the crazy things people ask us, like "It says to press any key. And I can't find the 'any' key." or "My computer isn't working," and we'll ask, "Is it plugged in?" and they'll say, "Yeah, it's plugged in the wall." "Well, did you move it?" "Yeah, I moved it yesterday." "Well, what about the other plug?" "Oh, you mean the gray one?" "Yeah, that one." "Oh, well that one wasn't long enough!" Just incredible stuff. One guy calls and says, "My cup holder's broken off." "What do you mean, your cup holder?" Well, come to find out it's the CD holder he was using as a coffee holder. Unbelievable! So stories like that at the beginning of a presentation are great, 'cause your audience says, "Gosh, I can't believe somebody's that stupid. Somebody's actually stupider than me!" They love it. They eat it up.

A feeling and a couple of thoughts are probably all they're going to take away from the presentation. That's been my experience. I suppose if you listen to Henry Kissinger talk you can walk away with the matrix of foreign policy. I remember listening to people like James Baker (former US Secretary of State) and walking away with a couple of thoughts. He put together some good anecdotes at the beginning of his speech that let you know that he was an expert and knew Mikhail Gorbachev. And then he said "This is what we've got to do, A, B, C."

I gave a speech recently to something called "The Masters" in Washington. It's the top 100 marketing executives from airline companies. They wanted me to talk about the Internet and technology. I usually try to use a couple of stories from my own life first, which resonates pretty well with people. I tell a story about technology. Someone once said, "Technology to you is whatever didn't exist when you were born." So a telephone is not technology to me but it would be to my great-grandfather. A computer is not technology to my kids. And that really came home to me when I was at a Boy Scout campout. We had an open fire with a cookout, and I said to one kid, "You're going to cook the bacon, so go get the bacon and get it ready." He came back and had the bacon wrapped in a paper towel. He'd never seen bacon cooked any other way than putting it in a microwave oven. So fire was technology to him. So I have a bunch of visuals to go through that story, but people go "Wow!" and then they begin to understand how their kids are going to deal with technology, the kind of technology that is here now, in a wholly different way. Will my kids be afraid to buy something on the Internet? Absolutely not. So people who run companies today have to understand where that generation is because we're building stuff for them now.

IN THE MIDDLE

The body of a presentation should first formulate a concept and then crystallize it with two or three key points. The audience will not remember every fact and figure heard during a speech, but they will retain at least one strong idea and a few substantial examples. Therefore, the speaker should stay away from pummeling his listeners with excessive data. Instead he should use Human Condition elements to explain the main topic.

Rick Dent: Take complicated information, break it down to its simplest form and communicate it. Philosophy courses taught me more about that than any English or history or journalism courses I ever took in college.

When speaking or pushing an issue, people today like to communicate with a laundry list because it's easy to do it that way and they think listeners can comprehend it. "I'm going to talk about three things today that are important to me. Number one: X. X has four parts. Number one, number two, number three, number four." What I tell all my clients is to forget that data. Forget that complex material. Speak from your heart and talk about why. That was the beauty of Ronald Reagan. He got criticized for not knowing all the details but people don't care about the details. They want to know about what motivates you, why you are interested in education. What it means to you and what it means to me. Not the intricate dialogue on education issues. When Reagan said "Tear down this wall," he didn't say, "Well, you know, first we've got to unite the two Germanys, and we'll probably have currency problems because right now they don't have shared currency, and then we've got Euro-dollars and how are we going to mess with that?" He simply said, "Tear the wall down, because people ought to be free." That's what people remember. And it's really the essence. Keep it simple, say it over and over again, and talk about why.

The idea of wrapping the entirety of a speech and all its key elements around the listener's interests and concerns seems logical enough, but is often forgotten or side-stepped by the speaker. The justification for violating such a simple rule usually revolves around the speaker's notion that he will be so commanding, so charming and dynamic, that the audience will forget who they are and what they believe to be important, and willingly follow like so many sheep. Wouldn't it be wonderful if life were that simple?

Rick Dent: One of my clients is the Atlanta Metropolitan Chamber of Commerce. Atlanta has the worst traffic situation in America and the longest commute of any city in America. That includes Los Angeles. It's thirty-six miles a day. There aren't enough highways and it's starting to kill the city.

So the Chamber of Commerce decided they were going to make transportation an issue for this next legislative session and they hired us to help them deliver that message. They wanted it to be complicated because it's a road building issue, and it has to do with air quality. And I went in there and basically did my job in one day. They said, "What should we talk about?" And I said, "Traffic." And they said, "Yeah, but that's not really the whole—" And I said, "Traffic." "Well why should we talk about traffic?" "Because that's what people are experiencing in their cars every day. That is what is impacting their lives. Air quality has no impact on them yet. Sure it's not what it used to be. And ten years from now it may be a health hazard. But no one is thinking about that right now when they're sitting in their cars for an hour. If you just say, 'We want to fix traffic' you will get their support." And it worked. But initially they looked at me like I was an idiot.

To their credit, we developed the message and it became a quality of life issue. "People can't get downtown to see a Braves game. It takes too long to get back home to pick up their kids before the daycare fines kick in. Fifteen-minute trips take an hour. We need to do something about it." In fact, the legislature just passed a major transportation initiative based on the work of the chamber, which started six months ago. And it's all about traffic. Because people want traffic fixed. They don't give a damn about air quality. Yet. Traffic they can understand. It was simple and it related to people's lives and the business community looked like they cared about their workers because it was about how they got around, not about creating jobs and economic development. And that was hard for them, cause they wanted to talk about jobs. And I said, "Look, you're making it about you. People don't give a damn about you lining your pockets. Let's talk about them." It was so simple.

So the main body of a speech must relate specific information, but that presentation should be filled with the Human Condition and relate directly to the audience. In so doing, it will appear that the speaker is invested in the subject matter as well as his listeners. The most fascinating communicators don't focus on pouring out data. They find ways to communicate their Quality Core through that data. Attaching one's core to the data humanizes it and makes it more palatable for the audience. As we said earlier, the speaker shouldn't expect the audience to feel any differently than he does.

Gary Chapman: The people that I admire and aspire to be like have an ability to immediately let you in. Amy Grant is like that. It's uncanny. In her case, it's a gift. Because she just doesn't think about it. She can be in a room with one person or ten thousand and every single one of them will be completely convinced that she is there only for them.

You can learn to find your core, but you can only find it if it's there. I'm finding now that I do have one. I know on a personal level that I've always had one. But on a public level I don't think I have. It's been very easy for me to dance through life with my humor crutch and deflect things away from sensitive areas. And I feel myself wanting to do that less and less. I still enjoy a laugh. But I more enjoy reality. If the laugh is reality, that's great. If the sadness is reality, that's great too. And this job has really helped me with that. I think everybody should have a talk show. That would be the best. We would all be better people. It forces you to find reality. Because the camera so instantly sees when you're fake and it deplores it. And by the same token, so instantly sees if you're real and applauds it. And for that I'm very grateful.

Don't read your speech! Obviously, I don't think I can say this enough. It's always amazing to me how many people in the public eye think that reading a speech will do just fine. Reading suggests that the author did not have the time or respect for those he is addressing to speak "from the heart." A speaker who delivers much of the presentation by reading it also loses credibility because there is no way of knowing who actually wrote those words. Although it is important that a presentation not ramble but be organized and concise, it must also appear to be conversational, and the speaker must appear to be connected to each and every listener.

Terry Jones: You've got to keep a pace and know where you are enough that you don't go off. Pace is critically important. Staying on target is also important, even if you have a very faint road map like just a bunch of slides. The problem a lot of people will get into is, someone will say, "I want you to give a fifteen-minute talk." Now it's hard for anyone to do a fifteen-minute talk, almost impossible. I usually won't do them. But sometimes you'll do it cause the audience is good enough. It's just so short that most people, if it isn't scripted, will go twenty-five or thirty minutes. And if you do that you're screwed.

Now staying on time is a great discipline, whether you're doing thirty minutes or forty-five minutes, to do it exactly on the second every time. Even though you don't have a script. You must pace yourself through the dot points and know what you want to say, and have just enough to say. I've seen many speakers get so into what they're doing they forget about that internal clock. And then they're stuck.

Understanding that talking to people is what they really want helped me a lot. They don't want speakers reading to them. There are so many who are so terrified that they write something out and they just read it. They don't have any fun and they don't make mistakes. And they're not human. And people hate that. It makes so much difference if you talk to them, not read at them. And just say, "This is what I want to talk to you about today."

• *Be a great storyteller, not a good reader.* Storytellers employ many techniques to keep the audience intrigued and on the edge of their seats. Some are inborn, most are learned, and all become natural elements inherent in the speaker's delivery over time and with a great deal of practice. Here are a few of the techniques that are basic building blocks for the great storyteller:

• *Energy*: Investing in a story to such a degree as to show an intense desire to communicate with the audience. Involvement is translated by eye contact and a strong voice. Energy has little to do with the volume or speed of delivery.

• *Tone*: The emotional quality of the voice—loving, harsh, compassionate, sarcastic—that sets the mood of a word, phrase or story.

• *Pitch*: How high or low the voice is on the "musical scale"— especially effective when delivering sentences containing parenthetical thoughts.

• *Stress*: Punching words. It can be particularly effective in pointing up contrast or opposition. One-word stress is greatly overused in presentations to achieve emphasis, frequently resulting in a singsong pattern.

• *Inflection*: Changing pitch within a single word. In phrasing, inflection helps to connect a key word to the rest of its modifiers; one-word stress will chop it off from its modifiers. Downward inflection is as effective as the more commonly used upward inflection.

- *Rate*: The speed at which words are delivered.

- *Pause*: It's not dead air! It is a purposeful stoppage of sound to attract attention or give emphasis. It's different from hesitation, which usually results in an "uh" verbalizing the pause.

- *Duration*: How long a sound is held.

- *Pace*: The dramatic ebb and flow of a story. A mere fast rate doesn't produce pace because it lacks contrast. To achieve *conversational pacing*, a person needs to vary the rate within the story and even within sentences, use effective pause, and employ appropriately varied duration.

- *Voice color*: Making words sound like what they mean in the context of the story. For example, shouting the word "loud" or whispering the word "soft."

Bill Taylor: A major element that goes into creating good communication would be vocal power. I'm going to throw in body language and gestures along with that power. All together, the drama of speaking. And that doesn't mean we all have to be a Clarence Darrow or some televangelist, but all of us have that ability to punch certain phrases or words and to pause for a moment, to make emphasis with gestures or emotions.

Rush Limbaugh is a great communicator. Although I know what he looks like and I know he wasn't that great on television, on radio he's absolutely fascinating. I may disagree with his stances and issues, but if you talk about the elements of good communication as all the arrows in a quiver, he uses every one of them every day. From the patronizing, the sweet-talking, the rage, the punch, the pause, every single thing you can think of he seems to put into his program.

The same can be said about Paul Harvey. He's an enormous communicator. He's the only appointment radio in my life. He's so effective. Students should spend a lot of time looking at the elements of what he does. You talk about the short declarative sentences, the punch and the pause. Understanding his audience and going to the heart of what they might be interested in. Or if they might not be interested, he makes it interesting, because he finds a way to write it, to tell it, to spin a yarn, to make it so that you get it. And that's communication. It's putting the audience first. Having the pulse of the audience.

VISUAL AIDS

It is true that the strongest element of communication is visual. Therefore visual aids should be considered when making a presentation. However, bear in mind that the strongest visual communicator is the human face, with its ability to create an endless number of expressions. After that comes body language. All other visual aids pale in comparison. Having said that, there are a few points to keep in mind when using external (other than face and body) visual aids:

- *Charts and graphs*   The use of visual aids makes statistical information more palatable. Keep in mind, however, that if the content of the presentation calls for an inordinate amount of these aids, it may be too laden with data and not enough Human Condition elements.

- *Do not distribute visual aids while speaking.*   Passing things around an audience is disruptive and distracting.

- *Expect the best and prepare for the worst.*   Rarely do live presentations go without a hitch, and usually that hitch involves some device connected with a visual demonstration. Always be prepared to deliver the same message without aids in case of mechanical failures or other disasters.

- *Make sure visuals are short and to the point.*   Graphics with many ideas or hard-to-read fonts only serve to distract the audience from your presentation. The rule of thumb is one idea per visual aid, and large, easy-to-read fonts.

- *Visual aids should support the speaker, not the other way around.* Don't make visual aids so complicated that time must be taken to explain them in detail. The visual aid should be self-explanatory and help to further the speaker's point.

There are countless techniques to support good storytelling in a presentation: Use the organization's name every so often; use the names of individuals in the group; use the word *we* instead of the word *you;* ask questions and solicit answers to further ideas and concepts; use visual aids; have the audience demonstrate concepts for themselves through group and individual exercises; and so on. The techniques are as varied as the speaker's imagination, and the cache of techniques grows with the detailed preparation of each new presentation.

In the End

You're in the homestretch. You've connected with your audience, entertained and enlightened them, and delivered your presentation so that they are energized and motivated. It's time to wrap things up and leave them with a sense of closure, answering any remaining questions and tying up all loose ends. The goal is to make sure the audience walks away sated.

- *Tell them where they've gone.* Summarize the presentation in a short paragraph.

- *Refer back to the beginning of your speech.* One way to give the audience a sense of closure is to complete the circle you started at the outset of the presentation. In other words, whatever device (story, statistic, etc.) you used to hook the audience up-front should be mentioned again or completed at the end.

- *Never introduce new concepts.* The final moments of a presentation are no time to give fresh information.

- *End strong!* The final thought should have as much energy and conviction as the opening statement.

- *End early!* Nothing makes an audience happier.

QUALITY KEYS

- *The five basic elements of a great public speaker are*: DNA, Quality Core, Human Condition, Techniques, and Practice.

- *Preparation*: Giving a speech without proper preparation will at the very least be nerve-racking, and could very well be devastating.

- *Think of the audience first!* What would the audience like to see and hear? What would the audience find interesting or funny?

- An audience will remember only a concept and a few main points of a presentation.

- Be a great storyteller, not a good reader.

- *The beginning*: Sets the mood and rhythm. It affords the audience a chance to get to know the speaker and affords the speaker an opportunity to get a read on his audience.

- *The middle*: The body of a presentation should first formulate a concept and then crystallize it with two or three key points.

- *The end*: It's time to wrap things up and leave the audience with a sense of closure, answering any remaining questions and tying up all loose ends.

10 ALL THE ANSWERS

HERE IT IS. THE MOMENT YOU'VE BEEN WAITING FOR. If you didn't cheat, and actually had the tenacity to read the entire book before peeking at these quiz answers from Chapter 1, it is appropriate at this time to congratulate yourself! Relish the moment. Go get yourself a cookie and celebrate your win. You deserve it. *Bravissimo!*[18] If you have, in fact, read up to this point, you probably already know these answers. If so, think of this chapter as review.

1. "I never said I thought you were crazy." This sentence has a definite element of —

e. Impossible to tell

Because it is out of context, the only way to know the exact meaning would be to hear and see it communicated by an individual. Since 93 percent of a person's communication is visual and tonal, this sentence could represent 800 different meanings.

2. The most powerful element of communication is —

a. Visual
Fifty-five percent of a person's communication relates to body language, facial expressions, hand gestures, grooming, clothes, surroundings, etc.

3. "I love you." This sentence can be verbalized how many different ways?
d. At least 50
Just by stressing a single word, there are at least three different meanings. Communicating with the Human Condition adds at least 100 different interpretations to each stressed word. Therefore, this sentence could actually have 300 different meanings.

4. Energy equals —
c. Investment
Investment brings out the best of one's core qualities and diminishes those characteristics that might get in the way of the communication process. Energy potential and the ability to wrap core qualities around communication are directly related to the investment a communicator has with the material.

5. What percentage of a person's communication comprehension is...?

38 %	Tonal	7 %	Text
55 %	Visual	100 %	Total

6. Marie Curie —
e. All of the above
During her study of radioactivity, for which she received a Nobel Prize, Marie Curie raised two daughters. She also discovered polonium and radium, for which she received a second Nobel Prize. One of Curie's daughters became an accomplished musician and author. The other daughter won a Nobel Prize for artificially producing radioactive substances by bombarding elements with alpha particles.

7. Who coined the phrase, "Float like a butterfly, sting like a bee!"?
d. Muhammad Ali

8. History's milestones —
a. Are stamped with the speeches of fascinating communicators.

9. Communicators are generally remembered for their —
c. Quality
Quality of character. Qualities of personality. The qualities from the core of the individual. The qualities that individual has attached to the work. Given a choice between the accomplished doctor who is technically proficient, and the accomplished doctor who really loves his job and has a great bedside manner, we will opt for the latter. What sets that professional apart from all the rest is his quality. It is how he performs his talent, not the talent alone.

10. Tertiary Core Characters make up —
d. The plethora of personalities marginally experienced over the course of a lifetime
…*TCCs* are not dominant, and usually take a conscious effort to call to the forefront of your core. The utilization of these personalities may take a stronger concentration but are still viable tools for the *communicator*.

11. The brain retains concepts by —
d. Attaching pictures and emotions
You might not remember what you had for lunch three days ago, but there are other events seared in your mind forever because of the vivid pictures and/or emotions attached to those memories.

12. The eyes are —
d. All of the above
The saying, "The eyes are the windows to the soul," reflects the fact that eyes register emotions through involuntary dilation and other characteristics.

13. The audience/viewers are always effected by —
a. The Human Condition

14. Intention is —
d. a & c. (A key element in learning and a key element in success.)

If your intention is to learn for practical application, you are more likely to retain that information. Also, successful individuals set short-term and long-term goals (intentions) with target dates to complete those goals.

15. The "Stanislavski Three" represent —
d. Questions the actor should answer regarding a character's existence
Stanislavski suggested an actor discover what his character is feeling inside, the manifestations of those feelings and the physical condition of the character.

16. "Ceiling Values" pose the questions —
a. "How much?" and "How pressing?"

17. In 1997, Troy Aikman took on a specialized coach for —
b. Basic quarterback skills
Wouldn't it be wonderful if everyone in our country had the same high regard for continuing education and self-improvement?

18. Uncontrollable tail wagging in cats signifies —
b. Acute conflict

19. 82% of TV viewers think reporters are —
c. Insensitive to people's pain

20. It is possible to be unbiased and —
d. Convey the Human Condition
If the story is written in a balanced fashion and you are true to the words, you can tell the story with feeling and still be objective, effective, and memorable.

WHAT'S THE POINT? REALLY!

Most men hate to make the bed. They see no reason for it. Why straighten the sheets, make hospital corners, fluff the pillows and tightly cover the whole thing with a bedspread you are then not allowed to sit on? (Makes me tired just thinking about it.) No one is going to see it during the day, and it is just going to get messy again in a few hours, so what's the point?

Years ago, I made that very argument to a girlfriend who became so exasperated with my logic she finally conceded with an offer to make dinner that evening. Full of myself for having won a significant victory for all men everywhere, I agreed to her peace offering.

That night at the dinner table, she presented me with nothing more than a large glass of brown liquid. At that moment I suddenly realized I had made the same fatal mistake every man makes, and every man has made in every relationship with a woman since the beginning of time: I actually thought I had won an argument.

"What is this? And what's that smell?" I asked.

(Second fatal mistake.)

"Dinner!" she exclaimed proudly.

"Yeah, but...what is it?" I questioned, really curious.

(Dumb, dumb, dumb!)

"Sushi. It's all the kinds you really like!" she said with a Cheshire grin.

Digging with all my might to assure that the hole I was about to fall into would be as deep as possible, I boldly continued, "I don't understand."

"I wanted to make your favorite," she said. Then a bit worried, "It is your favorite, isn't it?"

"You blended raw fish?" I asked, befuddled. (Because, apparently, protozoa have more brains than I do.)

"Not just raw fish, silly! Rice, seaweed, roe, and what's that stuff that's not really dead yet?. Oh, my gosh, I think I forgot and used the regular soy sauce instead of the low sodium."

"You blended raw fish?!"

Light began to dawn. My ship, however, began to sink. Gurgle.

She explained, "I thought about what you said this morning and, you know, you were right!"

Oh, yeah. The ship was definitely sinking. Gurgle...gurgle.

She continued, "Why take the time to make something look pretty when you know it's just going to get jumbled up anyway. I mean, what's the point? Really!"

Gurgle...gurgle...gurgle.

It's What I Do at the End of My Day

Well, what my lovely girlfriend taught me with the Neptune-shake from hell was that living for the moment is just not enough. We must keep the future in mind and prepare for it. For when we arrive, our present comfort and enjoyment will equal that of our past preparations.

Don't get me wrong. It is important that we enjoy the ride! Living life in present-time, having the ability to embrace each day and each moment as it comes, is the ultimate life experience. But we must find ways to invest part of our present-time energies in preparation for future experiences. "Making the bed" then becomes a metaphor for learning new and better ways to ply our trade, sharpen our skills and talents, spend quality time with children, teach others how to win, and so on. Now, if you can manage to enjoy these activities as much as eating, having sex, and shopping in Beverly Hills...well, remember when I said, "There is no Nirvana."? I lied.

I'm reminded of a client news director who still anchors the late-night news. A very nice man who had a fire for reporting and a fervency for anchoring when he started his career some twenty years ago. When we first met, I asked what role anchoring currently played in his life. His answer was chilling, yet the sentiment is all too common with many anchors.

He said, "Anchoring? It's what I do at the end of my day."

He spends his day managing staff, fielding calls, doing budgets, etc. He prepares for the show by looking at the run-down and writing a few stories. He might even read through a portion of the script before air-time. But anchoring is what he does at the end of his day. No real consideration of how the stories are to be delivered or what could be done to create fascinating communication. Never any time spent developing his skills as a communicator. After devoting a lifetime to the news, the newscast has become nothing more than a half-hour countdown to going home. To quote an old love, "What's the point? Really?"

ETHOS, LOGOS & PATHOS

It was Aristotle who said that every argument must have ethos (a central principal), logos (reason), and pathos (passion) to be complete. I submit that for a life's journey to be exciting, productive, challenging and fun, it must be composed of the same elements.

Ethos: A central principle, core idea or solid through-line.

The better understanding you have about the path you are on, the stronger your convictions will be to traverse it. Remember, "Knowledge is power!" Decide who you are and what you're about. Decide exactly where you want to go and why. Don't worry about making the wrong decisions. You can always change them if they don't work out. The most successful people make decisions and act on them. Those who vacillate end up being victims of circumstance.

Logos–Reason: Understanding your Ethos allows you to reason out short-term and long-term goals. Setting out to accomplish those goals puts you on the master's path. While traveling that road, you will be faced with many obstacles to contend with and decisions to be made. Having a solid understanding of where you are going will help you to overcome the obstacles and make the decisions that will keep you moving in the right direction.

Pathos–Passion: Enthusiasm, fire, excitement, desire, craving, fervency... I think you get the picture. Enjoy your work in present-time. Enjoy your family in present-time. Enjoy your life in present-time. You might not be in the best situation at the present moment, but going about it with Pathos can only help to better the experience and add value to the time spent.

TRADING DAYS

Each of us has only so many days to experience in this life. Most of us have the freedom and the ability to decide how we will spend those days. And all of us must be fully accountable for our current situations. We wake up every morning with the ability to choose where we will go, whom we will deal with and what we will aspire to. It is true that we all have present-time obligations and duties to perform. But it was our past decisions and actions that guided us to this point in time, helped formulate those obligations, and affirm those duties. Ultimately, we are all responsible for the life we lead. The bed you make today will be the bed you lie in tomorrow.

Even though the game of life does not allow you to store away time, but requires you to spend all of your days, you have the option of just giving them away or trading each one for the best choices you can make. Winning is not an accident. Success is never thrust on anyone. And "luck" really is the product of life's equation: "preparation plus opportunity."

Take a moment to think back on all the people interviewed in this book. All very successful, each one a wonderful communicator at the forefront of his or her particular craft, and in every case a fervent believer in the power of preparation and intention. All through grade-school I grew up hearing the platitude, "With hard work, persistence, moral values and a great attitude, you can do anything!" Well, there have been quite a few advancements since then: hand-held calculators, lap-top computers, video cameras, personal telephone answering machines, VCRs, cellular phones, the world-wide web, and so on. There is one thing that hasn't changed, however. That old grade school platitude. It is still a valuable lesson for our children and a key maxim for the Master Communicator.

You have the tools. You have the power. You have the ability to harness and utilize both. You have the privilege of choosing the road to Mastery, if you so desire.

Opportunity will definitely knock.

And if you feel you already missed opportunity, chances are it will knock again. The only question remaining: "Will you be ready when it does? Carpe diem!

QUALITY KEYS

- *Ethos — A central principle, core idea or solid through-line.* The better understanding you have about the path you are on, the stronger your convictions will be to traverse it.

- *Logos — Reason.* Continue to make the decisions that will keep you moving in the right direction.

- *Pathos — Passion.* Enthusiasm, fire, excitement, desire, craving, fervency … I think you get the picture.

Notes

1. Unless specified, definitions in this book are taken from the American Heritage Dictionary (American Heritage Publishing Co., Inc. 1969).
2. Webster's New Collegiate Dictionary (G. & C. Merriam Co. 1979) p. 596.
3. *KTBS*: The ABC affiliate in Shreveport, Louisiana.
4. *KD Studios*: An acting school founded in 1979 by Kim Dawson.
5. *Sandra Connell*: Currently president of Talent Dynamics, a Media Advisors International company specializing in talent placement and talent development for the broadcast and entertainment industries.
6. *Lucy Himstedt*: 1997 Chairman of the Radio and Television News Directors Association (RTNDA). News Director for NBC affiliate WSFA-TV in Montgomery, Alabama from 1992–1998 following two years as News Director for ABC affiliate KAIT-TV in Jonesboro, Ark. Himstedt spent the first ten years of her career at the CBS affiliate KTHV-TV in Little Rock, Ark.
7. *Vahan Moosekian* has produced a myriad of television films and series since 1984. His credits include the series *"Maloney," "Paper Dolls," " Tour of Duty,"* the Emmy winning movie *"Something About Amelia,"* and the Emmy nominated mini-series *"Child Lost Forever."*
8. Inaugural address, January, 1961.
9. See Ehninger, Gronbeck, Monroe, *Principles of Speech Communication* (Illinois: Scott, Foresman and Company, 1980): 72. Also see Albert Mehrabian, "Significance of Posture and Position in the Communication of Attitude and Status Relationships," *Psychological Bulletin* 71 (1969): 359-372.
10. *Audience Research & Development* is America's largest televisual research and consulting firm. Its clients include television stations, radio stations, newspapers, and film studios.
11. *model audience group*: A group of individuals representing the

socio-economic diversity of a region, brought together to watch and then comment on various television shows.

12. teaser: (Allan's description) "The first couple of pages of the script which usually has nothing to do with the story. It is a way to get people to watch from the top of the show."

13. Judith Valente (Parade Magazine, March 2, 1997): 4.

14. *Media Advisors International* provides strategic consulting and custom research services to the most successful and largest media corporations in the world. Its family of companies includes ASI Entertainment, AR&D, TV Strategy Group, Talent Dynamics, and Belden Associates.

15. *The "Peabody"* is the broadcast equivalent to the *Pulitzer Prize*.

16. In order to win the *DSA*, Shelby beat two runners-up, namely *Ted Koppel* and *Bill Moyers*.

17. *franchise*: Recurring news segment devoted to and highlighting the same subject, such as health, consumer issues or children, at least once each week.

18. Those of you who skipped to this page from Chapter 1...
    NO COOKIE!